D1582822

T...

PRACTICAL KINETOGRAPHY
LABAN

PRACTICAL KINETOGRAPHY LABAN

VALERIE PRESTON-DUNLOP, F.L.G.

Director of the Beechmont Movement Study Centre

MACDONALD & EVANS LTD
8 John Street, London W.C.1

1969

First published October 1969

©

MACDONALD AND EVANS LTD

1969

S.B.N. 7121 1609 5

Made and printed in Great Britain by
Fletcher & Son Ltd., Norwich, Norfolk

PREFACE

THIS book is intended as a textbook for people who are concerned with human movement, be they sportsmen, physical educationalists, dancers, research workers or ethnologists. It describes the method of writing down movement invented by Rudolf Laban, which is called "Kinetography Laban" in Europe and "Labanotation" in the U.S.A.

This is not the first book on the system. Laban, Albrecht Knust, Ann Hutchinson, Szentpal and Haas have all written textbooks, in either English, German, French or Hungarian. Why, then, write another? There are two reasons. Firstly, because previous books have been primarily geared to dance of various kinds, while the present book aims to supply information for a wider sphere of human movement. Secondly, I have developed a particular use of the system for writing only the outline of a movement on a simplified staff. This has been called Motif Writing. I put this idea forward in a booklet called *Introduction to Kinetography Laban* in 1963, and in *Readers in Kinetography Laban* in 1968 this was further explained. The present book sets out to show Motif Writing and Kinetography together and to form a study book between the *Introduction* and Knust's *Handbook* and *Encyclopaedia* and Hutchinson's *Labanotation*, which are the standard works. This book is not an exhaustive work, but it includes the essentials. The reader could hope to become an adequate writer and good reader of kinetograms of wide range by studying the contents, although it would require further study to become a first-class kinetographer.

The authoritative body on kinetography is the International Council of Kinetography Laban, and in preparing this book I have taken into account the Council's recommendations, including those of its conference in August 1967.

V. P.-D.

June 1969

ACKNOWLEDGMENTS

I HAVE had the good fortune to work with two great men. The first was Rudolf Laban, and my debt to him is immense. Not only did he create the system of Kinetography but he encouraged me as a student in such a way that I became able to take part in the exciting work of its development. The second is Albrecht Knust, with whom I continued my studies in Germany. He taught me what thoroughness and scholarship mean, and in this book his contributions to the system, and his particular way of organising the material, play a large part. Laban's inspiration and Knust's discipline have made my moderate talents into useful tools. I am also indebted to Ann Hutchinson, the Honorary President of the Dance Notation Bureau of New York, from whom I learnt American methods and whose practical point of view has tempered my academic leanings. My colleagues on the International Council of Kinetography Laban have helped me by making me clarify my own point of view. I am also grateful to Dartford College of Physical Education, especially the Vice-Principal, Mary Duggan, who enabled me to make kinetograms of students in action, and to Paddy Macmaster, who helped me in writing some of the kinetograms of work actions, and gave many suggestions on the text. The artwork for this book has been done by her and Mr T. Pucknell, and I am more than grateful for their painstaking efforts. Mrs I. Glaister has kindly allowed me to reproduce a kinetogram of a tennis stroke taken from one of her films, and Mr G. Adamson has given me permission to reproduce a tracing of one of his force platform graphs; I am grateful to them both. And I thank my husband John, who reads every word I write, deciphers every kinetogram I draw, corrects my English and never complains when, because of kinetographic ploys, I forget to cook the dinner.

CONTENTS

PRACTICAL KINETOGRAPHY LABAN

Chapter One

THE STAFFS, THE ACTION STROKE
AND RHYTHM

THE STAFFS

KINETOGRAPHIC symbols are written within a staff to show which parts of the body are moving.

The full staff is shown in **1**. This is further divided into columns **(1a)**. The centre two, known as the support columns, are used for steps, while the others are reserved for portions of the body. It is helpful to regard the centre line as representing the spine and the two outer lines as the waist. Everything for the waist downwards is written within the staff, while references for the waist upwards are written outside the staff. The broken lines are never written but are in the figure to facilitate understanding that the pairs of columns, reading from the centre outwards, are for supports, leg gestures, body movements and arm gestures.

2 is a simplified staff; it has only the central spine line and is therefore not capable of distinguishing between the upper and lower halves of the body. However, it does distinguish between the right side of the body and the left side. Its use is therefore limited to descriptions of movement which are very general, such as "move forward the whole of your right side" or "stretch the whole of your left side."

3 is another simplified staff. As it has neither spine nor waist lines, it is not capable, in itself, of describing the parts of the body which move. It is used to give a broad outline of what a movement is about, such as "sink down" or "turn around" or "stretch out."

The score is read from the bottom upwards. It always starts with a double bar line **(4)**, while a double bar line at the end indicates that the action is finished **(5)**.

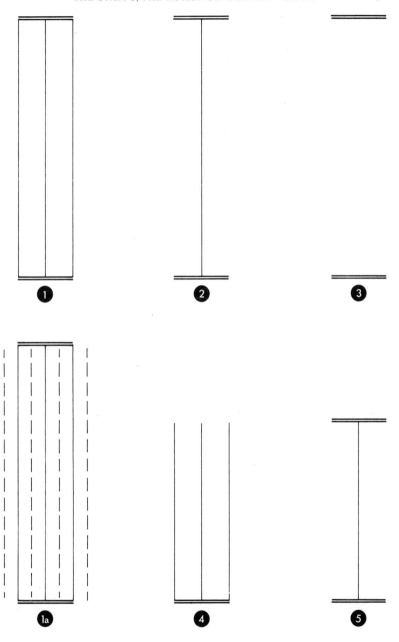

The time can be divided by bar lines, as in a musical score. In **6** three bars of 3/4 time are drawn out. In **7** there are three bars of irregular metre, one of 2/4, one of 4/4 and one of 3/4. In **8** the time to be used is divided in half. Below the double bar line space is left for the starting position **(9)**. This only has a single bar line at the beginning; time begins to run at the double bar line.

When more than one person is moving at the same time each staff is connected by a long horizontal line **(10)** at the beginning of the staff but not, note, at the end also.

One of the decisions that a kinetographer has to make when writing movement is which staff is suitable to his needs for the particular job in hand. It is likely that he will choose one staff for the entire job, but it is quite permissible to change from one staff to another if this proves to be the best way of describing the movement.

Let us say that the kinetographer is asked to write a detailed description of a dance study, or a gymnastic skill, or the action sequence of an industrial worker, or a long-jumper. He will obviously be interested in exactly what is done by each part of the body and will therefore, without hesitation, choose the full staff (**1**). But let us say that he is asked to record a lesson in creative movement for very young children, or the actions of a crowd in a play, or the outline for a dance before it is fully choreographed, or the main motions of a military parade; which staff should he choose? In any of these cases it would be very difficult, irrelevant or unnecessary to describe the actions of all parts of the body. The class of children will be moving quite individually, but with a common theme; the writer will therefore choose one of the simpler staffs **(2** or **3)** and write the theme in that. The crowd will also be moving individually, but within given limits and for a given purpose; again a simple staff will be the one to choose to describe these. The outline for a dance can obviously not be written in the full staff, but it may well be that brief fragments of it are clearly defined while the mass is a sketch. In this case the kinetographer will change from one staff to another as the need arises, for instance, using the full staff for a choreographed solo, but a simple staff for the unchoreographed movements of the accompanying group. Which of the two simple staffs is chosen depends entirely on whether the movement is for the body in general or whether or not an important distinction is made between the use of the sides of the body.

The reader has to learn to respond differently to the three staffs. His task when reading the full staff is fully to realise, in all detail,

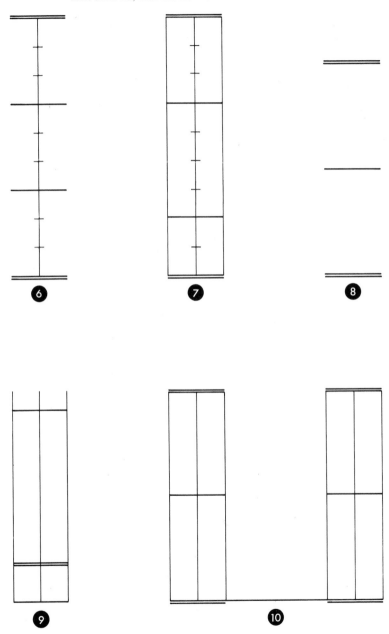

what is written and also to elicit the life of the action from the dead signs. This is vital, and it is most rewarding to find out not only what the exact movements are but what the spirit of the thing is, what it is all about. This is the reader's art. But when he reads a simple staff it is another matter, for he knows that only half the picture is given. This sort of writing either leaves scope for individual interpretation or relies on prior knowledge of the type of movement described. In the first case there may be ten different ways in which a written theme may be moved, and the reader's movement imagination needs to be put into play. In the second case the knowledge of, say, military arms drill, or a well-known athletic skill, has to be used. A score of this kind would only be useful to people with special knowledge and training behind them.

THE ACTION STROKE

Action is indicated by placing symbols within one of the staffs. The simplest symbol is the action stroke, simply a vertical line (11).

This symbol does not say what kind of movement is made, but simply that action of some kind takes place. In a full description the action stroke is rarely used, but it is useful for generalities. What kind of action does an action stroke indicate? Such things as bend- ing, arching, crumpling, stretching, closing in, rising up, leaning, twisting, punching, stamping, crouching and so on, dependent on the parts of the body involved. If only steps are indicated, they could be stamping, on the toes, large lunges, stepping well out, with stiff knees, bent knees, marking time. Leg gestures and arm gestures may be reaching out, contracting towards the body, twisting in and out, circling round, swinging to and fro, lifting up, across the body, away from it, bent, stretched. Movements of the upper part of the body may be leaning, bowing down, arching back, twisting, screwing round, stretching up and so on.

Read 12. Ten actions have taken place, the last two pairs happen- ing at the same time. What is known about the actions? They are steps and arm gestures. With which side of the body? Right, left, right, left in the steps, and right, left, both, both for the arms. Rhythm? Two bars of 4/4 time. Direction? Not known and therefore open to free choice.

Much less is known about **13**. What kind of action? Not known or free choice. With which side of the body? Right, left, right; both, both, left; both, both, right. Rhythm? Three bars of 3/4 time.

What does **14** describe? The answer is very simple—five actions of unknown kind and in unknown parts of the body. It tells you no more than that a rhythm of even beats is being brought out somehow in the body; little more is described than would be by the musical notes ♩ ♩ ♩ ♩ ♩ except that it is to be moved instead of sounded.

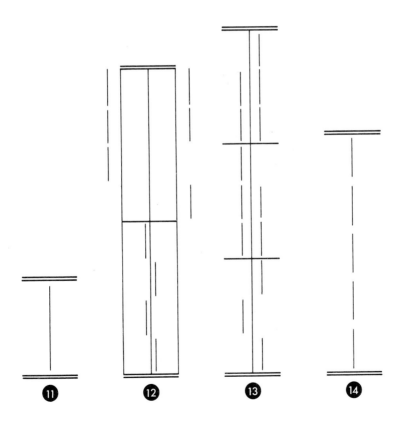

Look at **15**. What can be learnt about the movements described?

(*a*) We know the active parts of the body and whether steps or gestures are made. The sequence is step, step, leg gesture; step, step, step; step and gesture simultaneously three times, a kind of half-jumping movement; one step with three arm gestures; one step with three arm gestures, the part of the trunk above the waist participating also; finally, one step with both arms and both halves of the body moving, step, step.

(*b*) The side of the body used is known; the sequence is left, right, left; left, right, left; both three times; left; right; both, right, left.

(*c*) The rhythm of the movement is known; it happens on each even beat for six complete bars of 3/4 time.

(*d*) Direction? Unknown and therefore free choice.

As a reader how do you respond to this? With discipline concerning the active parts of the body and the rhythm, and with imagination concerning the direction and kind of action. How many ways of doing it are there? As many ways as you can think of.

Read it through twice, and then perform it without looking. You will find that your body will memorise the rhythm of the action without much difficulty. Check up by looking again and then move and try to find the overall "feel" of the phrase. You will find that the first three bars go together and concern leg movements, and that the second three go together and are mainly concerned with the upper half of the body. You may find that the first phrase has a general feeling of increasing activity, and the second of increasing body participation. In fact, from these few action strokes a movement phrase which is quite worth while can be invented, especially if imagination is used as to the kind of action which might be done.

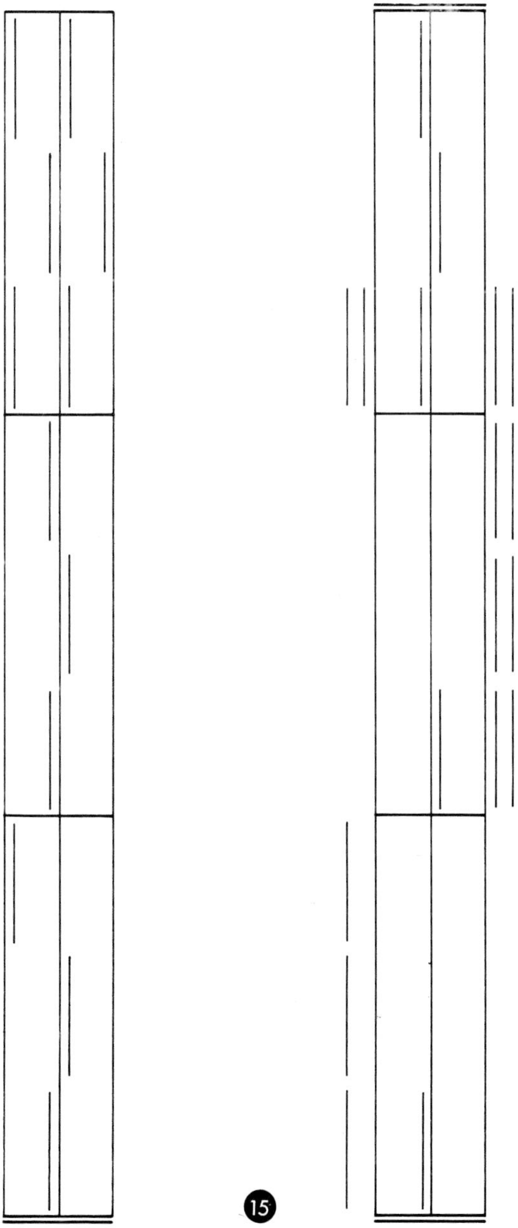

15

Look at **16a, b** and **c**, and find out what you can about them.

(*a*) The long horizontal line joining the three staffs shows that there are three people moving simultaneously.

(*b*) There is a starting position for each mover; movers "**a**" and "**b**" start with the weight on their left foot and mover "**c**" has the weight on both feet.

(*c*) The rhythm of each mover is identical, but they produce this rhythm by making different kinds of actions and using different parts of the body. The rhythm consists of four even beats to each bar.

(*d*) Mover "**a**" uses steps only in the first two bars. In the third and fourth bar the same step rhythm is repeated, with arm gestures.

(*e*) Mover "**b**" uses the legs only, and is the only one of the three to use gestures of the legs. The first two bars are repeated in the third and fourth bars, but on the other side of the body.

(*f*) Mover "**c**" uses steps only in the second bar, the main actions being in the arms and the upper part of the body.

Nothing is said about the direction and size of the steps or the direction and extension of the gestures, nor about the relative positions of the three movers. Many interpretations could be made, which could result in interesting relationships between the three movers.

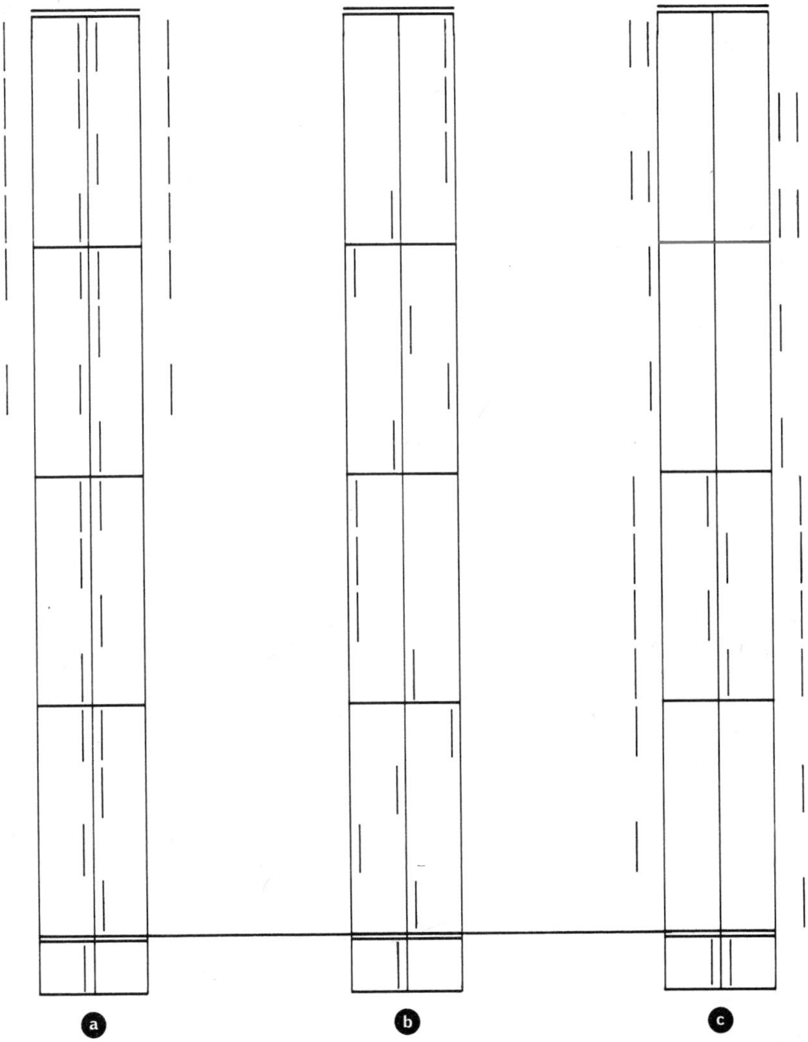

16

DURATION AND RHYTHM

The duration of the movement is shown by the length of the action stroke, a long stroke indicating a slow movement, and a short stroke indicating a brief movement **(17)**.

The juxtaposition of slow and brief actions brings about rhythmical movement. There are two kinds of rhythm in movement, that derived from a regular pulse, and that derived from action. The former is usually called *metric rhythm* and is based on a time unit which is constant throughout the movement and which can be divided into half units, and quarter units, or multiplied into double units, etc. It is used in dance a great deal, particularly in folk dance, also in marching and in any movement closely allied to some accompanying music. The other kind of rhythm is usually called *action rhythm*, sometimes *breath rhythm*, but it is essentially rhythm which is not linked with a metric unit and is free of numerical divisions of time. This is the rhythm used in everyday actions, in speech, in sport or in most working action sequences.

Movements in metric rhythm are easier to write down than those in action rhythm, because the length of a time unit can be decided upon at the start by the writer. All he has to do is to see that the length of the symbols correspond to the duration of the movement, which may be for two units or half a unit or whatever is the case. **18** shows a scale of relative lengths and gives the corresponding time unit in the musical equivalent. Action rhythms require more thought in that each action or part of an action has to be compared with others to ascertain whether it is shorter or longer than the one before, and how much shorter or longer; the symbols must then be adjusted accordingly. In certain cases, such as the comparison of the actions of two workers on the same industrial job, absolute accuracy is essential and then there is nothing for it but the stop-watch.

19 shows a typical use of metric rhythm in steps. The musical notation would be:

20 shows a typical use of action rhythm in steps. There is no exact musical equivalent, but something like this might do:

The phrase is obviously stepping with increasing speed to very fast, ending with one slow step; no movement for a long time, and at the last minute two steps, one brief and one slow.

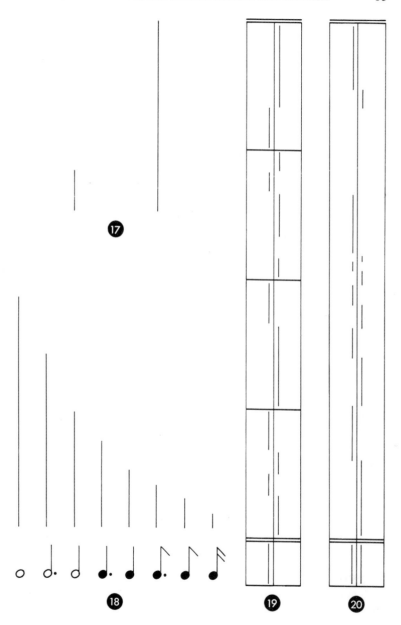

CESSATION OF MOVEMENT AND
THE RETENTION SIGN

Another feature of the rhythm of action is that it includes pauses. These are indicated in most cases by a lack of symbol; if nothing is written do nothing. But in the case of the support column this simple device does not function. Why not? Because a step is not a gesture but a transference of weight; if a gap in a gesture column means "do not make a gesture," a gap in the support column means "do not support," which does not mean pause but, rather, quite the opposite; it means jump, lose your support, be airborne not floor borne.

A basic rule of kinetography therefore is that a gap between symbols in the arm and upper part of the body columns indicates a pause, and a gap in both support columns indicates a jump.

21 illustrates this rule. The action is step, leap, leap; the arms move, pause and move again.

Something therefore has to be used to indicate that the weight is retained on the leg if a pause is to be made and not a jump. This is the *retention sign*, a little circle.

In a simple staff the retention sign is always used to show that a position is retained, that the mover pauses. **22** shows that positions resulting from the first and third movements are held still for a short while.

In **23** the third action, which is made by the right side of the body, is held while the left side moves; finally, both sides are still.

24 illustrates three occasions for which the retention sign is necessary in the full staff. The first is when keeping the weight on one foot; without it a jump would be indicated. The second is while a leg gesture is being made; without, it would show a jump while gesturing. The third is when keeping the weight on one foot while stepping on to the other; without it the weight would be completely transferred, but with it the weight is finally evenly distributed between the two legs.

25 shows how no retention signs are necessary in the arm gesture column to show that the position is held; this happens automatically. It also shows how retention signs are put in the support columns to mean standing still.

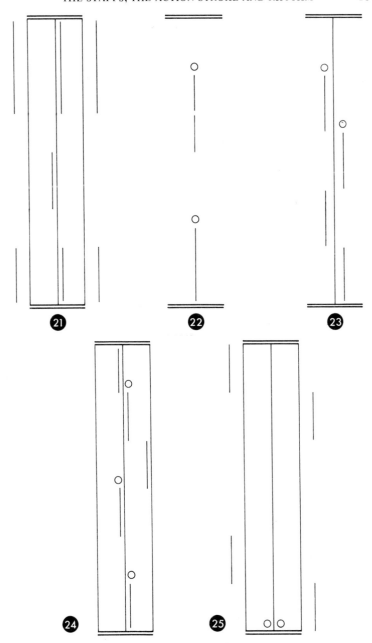

It will now be appreciated that some of the earlier examples in this book are, in fact, incorrectly written, as a gap has been described generally as a pause. You would be in a position now to look through **12**, **15**, **16** and **20**, and correct them by inserting retention signs.

Read **26** to **29**, and move them, paying particular attention to the duration and pauses. They are all examples of rhythmical movement. **26** to **28** are in metric rhythm, but **29** is in action rhythm. It is customary to put a time signature on the left side of the first bar of a staff in metric rhythm; in **27** each beat has been indicated to facilitate correct reading of the rhythm.

26 uses steps and arm gestures;

27 involves the two halves of the body;

28 requires both steps and leg gestures;

29 uses steps, leg gestures, body movements and arm gestures.

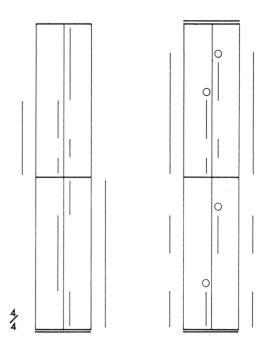

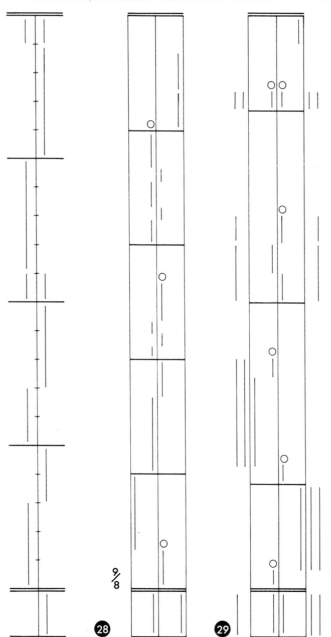

$\frac{9}{8}$

27

28

29

JUMPING

A gap in both support columns means a jump. There are five basic ways of jumping, and they are shown in **30–34**.

30 is from one foot to the same foot, hopping.

31 is from one foot to the other foot, leaping.

32 is from one foot to both feet.

33 is from both feet to one foot.

34 is from both feet to both feet.

30–33 could also be done on the other side.

In the simple staff a special device has to be used to show jumping. This is because there is no distinction between supports and gestures and a gap in the simple staff, as in **35**, is meaningless. Therefore the two actions made in a jump, the take-off and the landing, are linked together by vertical brackets, as in **36**.

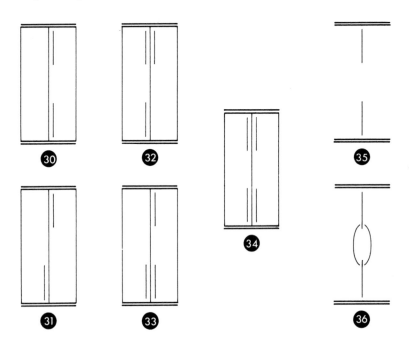

The rhythm of jumping is affected by the size of the jump, as the bigger the jump, the longer the time needed to do it. This is shown by the length of the gap between the take-off and the landing.

37a–c show jumps of varying sizes written in the full staff.

> **a** shows running, when the amount of time in the air is quite short.
>
> **b** shows bounding along, with a longer time in the air.
>
> **c** shows big leaps, with the time in the air longer than on the floor.

38 shows four jumps, increasing in size, written in the simple staff.

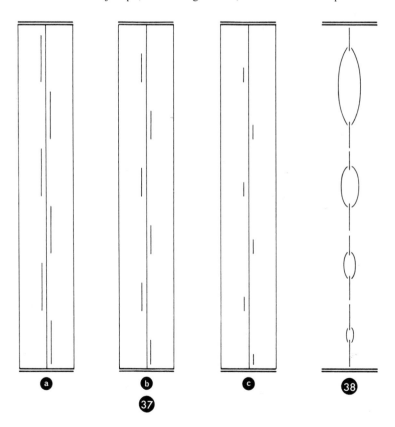

The kinetographer has to record the relationship of the time in the air to the time on the ground and draw his symbols accordingly. This is particularly so when the jump is not in a dance sequence which has a metric rhythm, but is something like an athletic skill or a gymnastic sequence or a dance movement where the rhythm is determined by the mover and not by the accompanying music.

Jumps in metric dance have typical rhythms which occur again and again, especially in folk dance or ballet. The kinetographer needs to be well acquainted with these so that they can be written quickly and easily. **39–42** are examples of skipping; the first two occur very often and the second two rarely.

> **39** is skipping in 3/4 time. Note that the step is on beat one, the flight on beat two and the landing on beat three. This is a typical skipping rhythm in triple time.
>
> **40** is skipping in 2/4 time. Note that the take-off step is shorter than the landing one, and the time in the air is quite brief. This is typical of skipping in duple time and produces a rather heavy action with the emphasis on the landing.
>
> **41** is an unusual rhythm for skipping, as it produces a syncopated action. Note that the landing does not occur until two *and*. Many a beginner writes this mistakenly instead of **40**.
>
> **42** again is unusual, but is what happens when the skip is energetically performed with considerable elevation.

43–45 are examples of jumping.

> **43** shows the typical way of jumping in 2/4 time. Note the landing is on the beat, which is usual.
>
> **44** shows a less typical way of jumping. The landing is on the off-beat, producing a syncopated action. The emphasis is on the elevation which occurs on the beat.
>
> **45** is an example of what is written when the first action of all is a jump. The elevation is on the last beat of the preceding bar, and therefore this up-beat is written after the starting-position graph.

Some writers have a little difficulty in analysing the rhythm of jumps to start with, but if the point in time of the landing is noted as first priority the difficulties are likely to be short-lived.

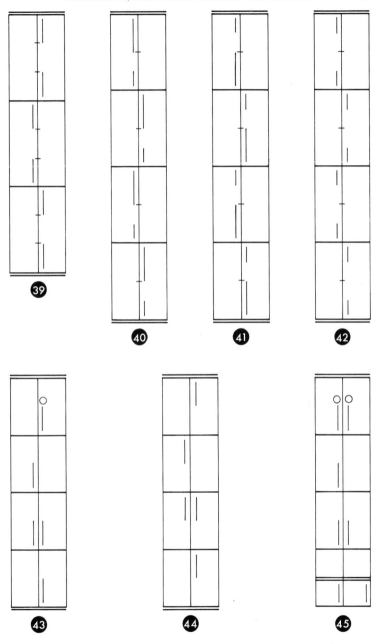

LEG GESTURE RHYTHMS

It is also important for the kinetographer to be aware of the rhythms used in leg gestures, and to note the use of the retention sign.

46. The retention sign is needed in the first and last bars; the rhythm of leg gesture and landing occurring together is a typical one.

47. Note the use of the up-beat for the preparatory gesture. This often occurs at the beginning of a movement sequence, particularly if the starting position is on both feet.

48. Note the timing of the gesture in relation to the transference of weight. The rhythms shown in bars 1 and 2 are often found, the first giving a rather deliberate gesture and the second a more fluent trans-ference-gesture rhythm. Bar 1 is typical for a gesture which is made into a new direction, while bar 2 is typical for a gesture resulting from a step. Bar 3 shows an even more fluent gesture which happens while transference is still going on. Bar 4 shows a movement which is a mixture between a step and a jump as the transference and the gesture occur simultaneously; it is found quite frequently in some folk dances, but hardly ever in everyday actions. It can be performed only in a fairly fast tempo.

49. This shows three hops and two leaps in which the actions of the legs during the jumps are important. In bar 1 the free leg, that is the leg not actively engaged in jumping, is important prior to and during the actual period in the air. This is typical of a gesture which helps to propel the body up or along. In bar 2 the free leg is not especially active until the point of landing. In bar 3 both legs are active during the jump, the free leg starting to move before the jumping leg. The free leg makes a second movement during the landing. In bar 4 the right leg is especially active during the period in the air, and in bar 5 the left leg is also important just before and during the landing. This last is very typical of large leaps.

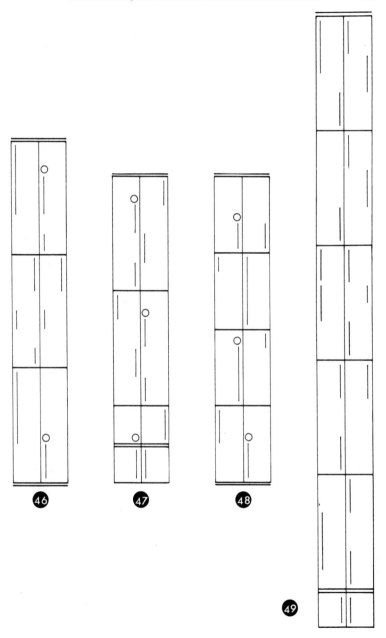

46   47   48   49

Read **50.** It is a sequence in which action strokes occur in all the columns so that the rhythm of the action in the whole body is absolutely clear. Any directions may be used by the reader and any size of movement. Note first the metre of the bars. Note also that during the 3/4 bars the movements are slower than during the 4/4 and 2/4 bars. Here the movements are sharp and the flow is stopped after each step. In bar one the arms move sharply with the first step and then hold still. In the second bar only the right arm gives up its position in the flowing hop and the body participates with the arm. Note the gesture of the left leg. The third bar is a shorter repeat of the first, but with body participation. The fourth bar is a repeat, on the other side, of the second bar, and the last one is an energetic movement involving the whole body in a jump on to both feet after both legs have gestured.

Read **51.** This is a sequence of eight bars which is rhythmically tricky, as it includes both typical and syncopated body rhythm and also brings in triple rhythms. Read it slowly first and then try to speed up, as it is best performed fairly fast. It can be repeated on the other side.

NOTE:

(i) In bar two the two leaps are syncopated, in that the landing of both is on the off-beat.

(ii) Bar three is a development of bar one, in that a triple rhythm is introduced in the third beat.

(iii) In bar four the last movement of all is a jump. The right leg gesture cancels the retention of weight sign.

(iv) In bar five the last movement is a very brief jump.

(v) Bar six is a development of bar five, including a triple rhythm at the end.

(vi) Bar seven is a repeat of bar four.

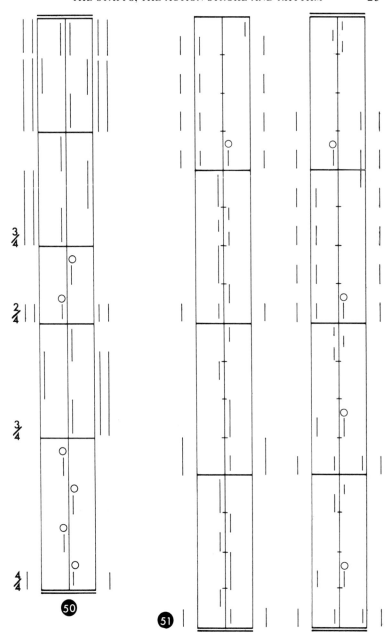

Chapter Two

DIRECTIONAL INDICATIONS

MAJOR DIRECTION SIGNS

THE direction and level of a movement are shown by an elaboration of the action stroke. The shape given to the stroke shows the direction of the movement. The four basic shapes are shown in **52a–d**.

> **a** is used for vertical movement;
> **b** for forward and backward movement;
> **c** for sideways movement; and
> **d** for diagonal movement.

53 shows the nine basic directions: centre, forward, backward, right, left, and the four diagonal directions, right-forward, left-forward, right-backward and left-backward.

The direction signs are used in exactly the same way as the action stroke.

54 shows general movement into five directions.

55 shows the same directions, but indicates which side of the body is to predominate during the movement.

Direction signs in the full staff show which part of the body is making the action, and that this action is clear directionally.

Look at **56**. The direction signs are in the support columns and replace action strokes. The rhythm is /ta ta ta-aa/, four times, and then two bars of /ta ta ta ta/. In the forward and backward steps, note that the long side of the symbol is placed nearest to the centre line. This is always done so that in fact there are two symbols for forwards and two for backwards. In the staff with no centre line either can be used. In the second bar the movement is all to the left, the first and third steps being open ones, the second one being a crossing-over step. The fourth bar is all to the right, stepping across, open and across. These four bars make a square floor pattern. The last two bars are diagonal steps, two into each direction, and they make a diamond floor pattern.

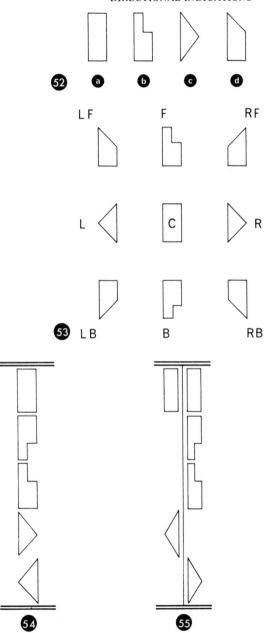

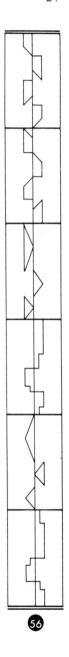

52

a   b   c   d

L F   F   R F

L   C   R

53 L B   B   R B

54   55   56

57. Note the way of writing a step beside the other foot. The action is: forwards, forwards, close the feet and pause on both; step open to the left and bring the right foot to the left foot, twice, pausing with weight on the right only; three steps on the spot, marking time.

58. The legs gesture forwards and then backwards, round in a half circle, and then shoot out diagonally forwards and backwards. Action strokes are used for the steps, as their direction does not matter in this instance.

59. The arms move forwards and open to the side, one after the other, and then swing to and fro round the body.

60. The upper part of the body bends to either side, leans forward, arches back and twists round, first to the right and then to the left.

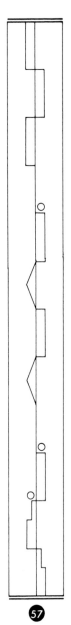

57

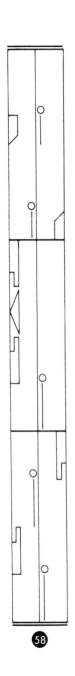

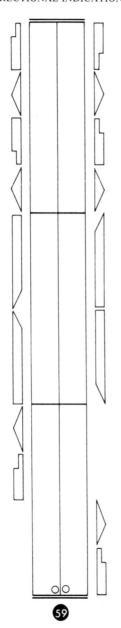

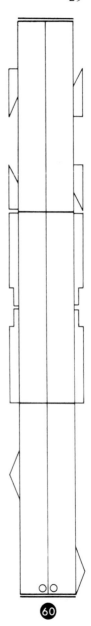

58 59 60

While the main direction is shown by the *shape* of the sign, the level of the direction is shown by the *shading* of the sign. The three levels are shown in **61**.

The striped sign shows the high level.
The dotted sign shows the medium level.
The blacked-in sign shows the deep level.

Between them, the shape and the shading give the twenty-seven directions shown in **62**.

It is helpful to divide the directions up into three groups: *see* **63–65**.

63 shows the ones which are known as the *dimensional* directions. The sequence starts in the central direction. The directions are then vertically upwards and vertically downwards, horizontally to the right and the left, and horizontally forwards and backwards.

64 shows the *diagonal* directions, which are those that would reach to the corners of a cube. They are drawn in pairs of opposites in this example, starting with the corner which is high in front and to the right.

65 shows the directions *between* the dimensionals and the diagonals; these would reach the middle of the edges of a cube. The first bar shows the directions in the frontal plane, the second bar those in the horizontal plane, and the third those in the sagittal plane.

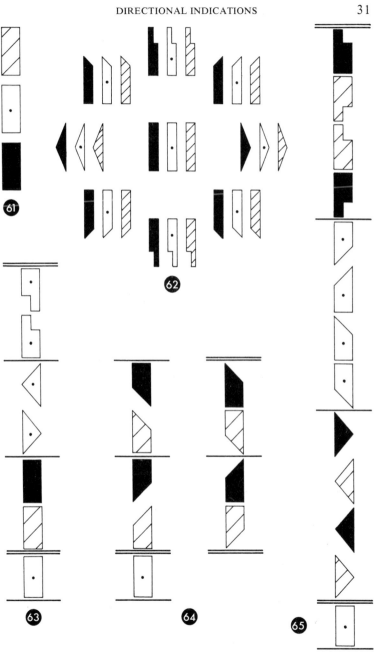

IN THE SIMPLE STAFFS

When direction signs are used in either of the simple staffs the level and direction are judged from the centre of the body, as the movement is a general whole-body expression. The centre of the body is called "place," the place of origin of the movement. In **66** and **67** the signs are used in this way.

66 indicates that the body rises, sinks, moves right-forward, left-backward, forward-upward, backward-downward, to the left, to the right and to place. It should be read with discipline as regards direction, but with imagination as to the kind of way the body uses the direction. Steps, leg gestures and the participation of the upper part of the body can all be used inventively. Note the starting position and the last movement. The latter says, "Come to the place of origin, the body centre," and will involve some sort of contracting movement towards the waist area.

67 shows a simple directional sequence performed first with the right side predominant and then, after a symmetric transition in "place," with the left predominant.

In **68** the signs for direction and jumping are combined. The directions do not mean simply the direction of the jump but the directional actions of the body while jumping. In the first jump the body uses the forward horizontal direction, in the second the two sideways directions and the last jumps are from left-forwards to vertically deep to right-forwards to vertically deep.

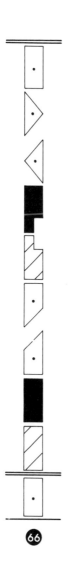

66

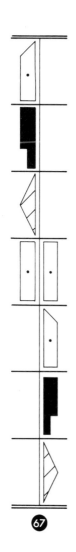

67

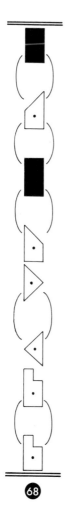

68

IN THE FULL STAFF

The level of movement is understood in different ways according to the action and parts of the body involved, but these ways are quite simple to learn.

(*a*) *For steps.* **69** shows forward steps in the three levels. Medium steps are normal steps, on the whole foot and with knees more or less straight at the end of the step. High steps are performed well up on the balls of the feet, with stretched but not stiff knees. Deep steps are performed on the whole foot and with knees bent as far as they can go without lifting the heels or straining the thighs.

The level of movement can alter during a transference of weight, and a kinetographer should be able to recognise the difference between the examples in **70**. The transference is completed in the deep level in the first bar; in the second bar the transference is not completed until the high level is reached.

When jumping, the knees give at the moment of take-off and landing. There is a question, therefore, as to which level should be given to these actions. It is a question of degree, for in most cases the level is somewhere between medium and deep.

71 shows an example of leaping movements in which the time in the air is quite short, and therefore the amount of propulsion needed is quite small. The level is therefore written as medium, as the knee bend is negligible, just enough to get off the ground.

72 shows leaps with a longer flight time, needing greater propulsion and therefore much knee bend. Deep level is used to convey this.

73 shows running on the toes. There will be a slight knee bend, but the main feeling is of lifting up, which the high level best conveys.

Read **74**. It is a sixteen-bar sequence of steps and jumps in 3/4 time. Move it and try to perform it finally without looking at the script.

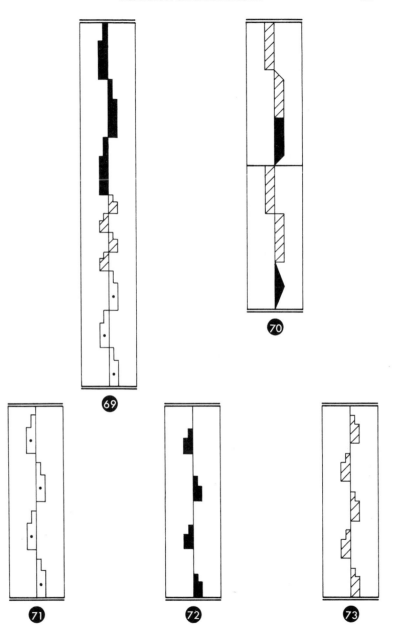

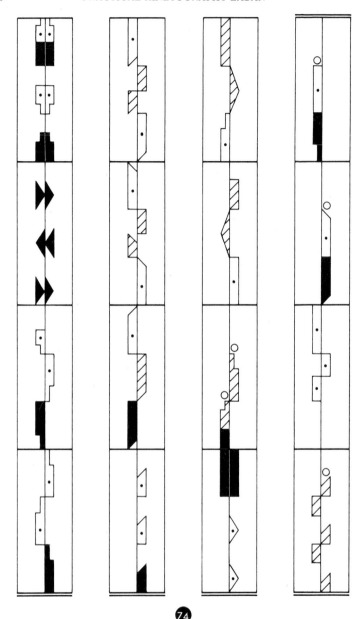

3/4

74

(*b*) *For leg gestures*. The level for leg and arm gestures is judged in quite another way. The joint which originates the movement is taken as "place," and all directions and levels are judged from there. So for leg gestures the level is judged as follows:

> deep level is below hip level;
> medium level is at hip level;
> high level is above hip level.

75 illustrates this in a sideways leg gesture. Most people cannot get their leg above medium level, but dancers and acrobats can and do frequently. Most leg gestures are below hip level, and therefore the kinetographer will expect to have many deep-level gestures in his graphs. Look at **76a–c**.

a. This shows deep leg gestures during jumps.
b. Note the vertical deep gestures; the left leg will pass by the supporting leg.
c. Note the gesture in place, which will mean a contraction of the leg.

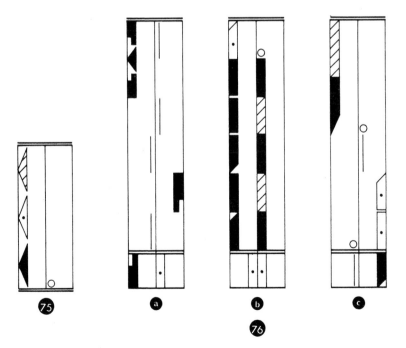

Look at **77**. The steps and gestures are clearly expressed in detail. Note the right-leg gesture in the last beat of the seventh bar. It starts on the up-beat, creates a jump and makes the landing on the left on the first beat of the next bar.

Read **78**. This is a sequence of steps, leg gestures and jumps. Try to memorise it so that you can perform it without looking at the script.

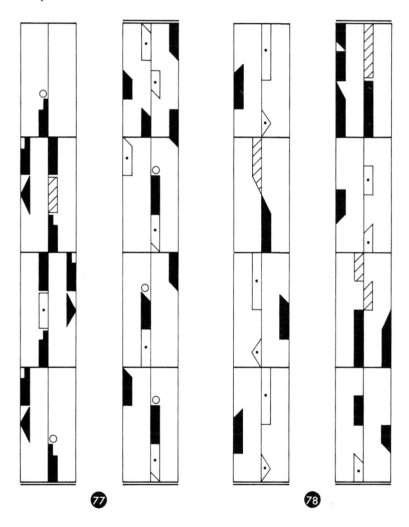

77   78

(c) *For arm gestures.* The level of arm gestures is judged from the shoulder; therefore:

deep level is below shoulder level;
medium level is at shoulder level;
high level is above shoulder level.

79. This illustrates the three levels in forwards and sideways directions.

80. Vertically down is the normal position of the arms at rest by the sides of the body. "Place" means bring the arms in to the shoulders. Vertically up brings the arms above the shoulders.

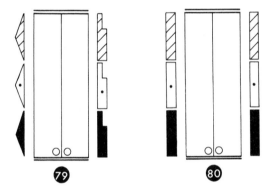

81. Note that the forward direction for the arm means directly in front of the shoulder, not in front of the chest. A special device is used for this which is explained later in this chapter.

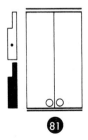

82 is a sequence of arm movements. The kinetographer must not be content just to recognise the symbols and be able to perform them. The reader's art is to find out the movement sense. In this sequence the right arm moves and is joined by the left. The right gathers across above the left, and swings back to sideways-deep as the left swings right round in a spiral.

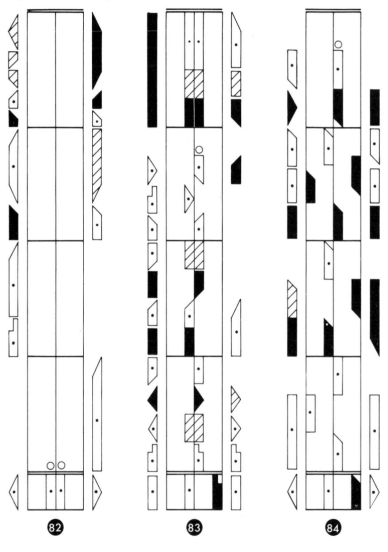

82   83   84

83 includes steps and arm gestures. The arms begin with the hands closed in to the shoulders. When the right arm reaches high to the right it holds that position as the left arm moves left-back in preparation for the swing across, where it meets the right arm. The right arm then stays as the left swings back and horizontally round. The right lowers a little so that the left can pass above it as it closes across. As the right sweeps over the top, the left slowly lowers down to be beside the trunk.

84 includes jumping, leg gestures and arm gestures. It has a swinging rhythm and should be performed with verve. Although no movement is indicated for the trunk or chest, it is evident that these parts must move in the last bar, as the left arm cannot reach the direction right-back without the body twisting to allow it to do so.

(*d*) *For upper part of the body movements.* Direction signs in the third column, that is between the leg- and arm-gesture columns, indicate movements of the upper part of the body. There is no one point of origin of the movement, as the spine is made up of many vertebrae. How does the kinetographer judge the direction and level of such movement? As there is no "place," there can be no above it for high level, and below it for deep level. Laban first had the brilliant idea of how to solve this problem, and Albrecht Knust has further developed it. Knust considers upper part of the body movements in relation to arm movements, as it is usually in response to these that the body moves.

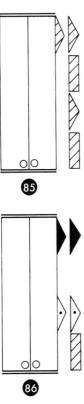

85 illustrates a movement performed with the arms only and then with participation of the upper part of the body, which tilts to the side a little. In **86** it also tilts, but a little more and then even more. So what does the level indicate? It shows how much of the upper part of the body is involved, how far down the spine and about how many vertebrae are moved.

It would not be helpful to calculate exactly how many vertebrae are involved, as, even if one knew, one could not control the spine to the necessary degree. But it may be said that high-level movements involve the top of the spine, medium-level involve the rib cage, and deep-level involve the whole of the dorsal spine and the waist area.

Having grasped that the level decides the amount of spine involvement, let us see what the direction indicates. It is advisable to perform upper part of the body movements with an arm movement into the same direction. The movement meant then becomes quite clear, particularly if you take a starting position with the arm vertically above the shoulder as in **85** and **86**.

Look at **87a–c**, which concern sideways directions.

> **a** and **b** both show lateral bending movements.
> **c** is not possible as the bends cancel each other out.

88a–c are concerned with forward directions.

> **a.** This shows that the right half of the body goes forward. It is a complex movement consisting of a slight twist and slight rounding of the back, as if accompanying a forward arm gesture.
> **b.** This is similar to **a.**
> **c.** Here *both* sides go forward and a simple bending of the spine forward results.

89a and **b** both show a complex movement, a mixture of a twist and an arching of the spine. But **89c** is a simple arching movement, as both sides of the body go back.

90a and **b** are also a mixture of twisting and bending, or leaning, but there is less twist in a diagonal movement than in a forward or backward movement. This is clearly shown in **91**, in that the movement is first leaning only, then leaning and twisting a little and then leaning and twisting quite a bit, all accompanying the arm gesture. **90c** is never written, as the resulting movement would be a simple arch and bend best expressed by **89c** and **88c**.

To sum up so far:

> (i) Lateral bending is indicated by a sideways direction sign in one of the body columns.
> (ii) Arching the back is indicated by backwards direction signs in both body columns.
> (iii) Bowing forwards is indicated by forward direction signs in both body columns.
> (iv) Mixtures of the above with twisting are shown by a forwards, backwards or diagonal sign in one of the body columns.
> (v) The amount of spine involvement is shown by the level of the signs.

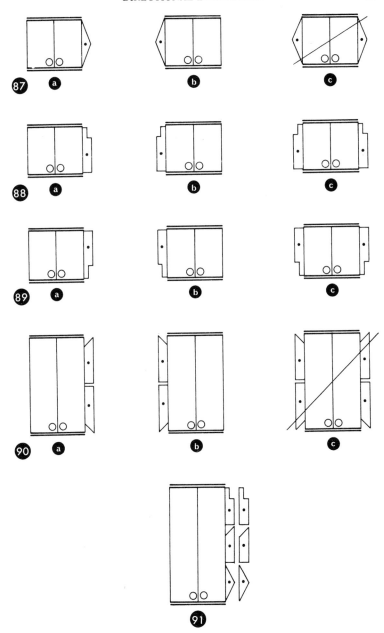

Looking at **92a–c**, let us see what opposite direction signs in the body columns produce.

> **a** is impossible.
> **b** produces a 90° twist with no bend.
> **c** produces only a 45° twist and again no bend.

The level in simple twisting movement is immaterial, as the amount of spine used is an integral part of the degree of twist, a 90° turn requiring participation of the whole dorsal spine and waist area.

In **93** opposite directions and levels are shown.

> **a** and **b** are similar; in both a double sideways indication is possible. The only difference is that in **a** the left side of the body is also active and lifts.
> **c** and **d** show a twist, but the right shoulder is lower than the left, so that a bend occurs too.

In **94a** and **b** both sides of the body go into the same direction. The result is a leaning movement, with no twist.

95a–d show the last direction signs to be considered. They have special meanings as follows:

> **a** and **b** do not mean a lift or stretch of any kind because "vertical high" is considered to be the normal carriage for the upper part of the body. They are used to show "return to the normal carriage," from either a one-sided or double-sided body movement.
> **c** and **d** are not used as these directions have no clear meaning for the upper part of the body.

96a–g summarise the upper part of the body movements.

> **a** shows normal carriage of the upper part of the body.
> **b** and **c** show lateral bending.
> **d** shows rounding forwards.
> **e** shows arching backwards.
> **f** and **g** show twisting.

Any other direction, either one-sided or double-sided, describes a movement which is a mixture of these actions.

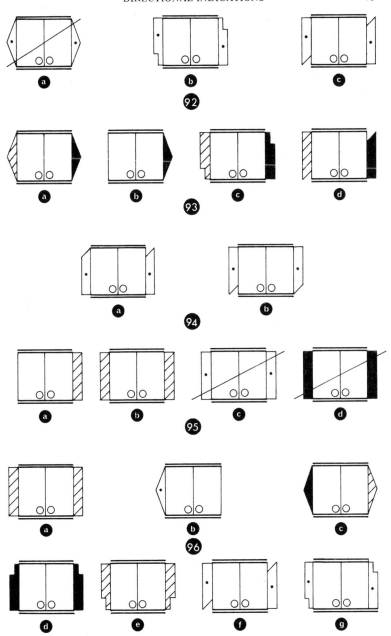

The upper part of the body often moves as a natural accompaniment to an arm gesture, particularly in everyday actions and spontaneous movement. In these cases there is an easier way of describing the body movement than writing direction symbols in the body columns.

Compare **97a** and **b**. The vertical bracket in **b** can be used instead of the direction sign in **a**, because the movement of the upper part of the body is a simple participation in the arm action, with a certain amount of freedom allowed. If the participation is obviously more than normal, **97c**, less than normal, **97d**, or into a different direction, **97e**, then it must, of course, be written out fully.

The kinetographer has to remember that a direction sign in the body column is valid until another direction sign for either the same or the other half of the body is written. If the body has been leaning and then comes back to its normal carriage a "vertical high" sign is written. In **98** the lean to the right is cancelled by the backwards movement of the left side, which is cancelled by the forward bend, and the body finally comes back to normal.

99 shows two other methods which can be used to describe the return to the normal carriage of the body. The first is the decrease sign, similar to the *decrescendo* sign in music. The second sign, a circle with a dot in the middle, is called the "return to normal" sign and is the creation of the New York Dance Notation Bureau. It is rarely used in European scores, but it is a very useful sign and may well become more widely used.

If an upper part of the body movement is shown by a bracket, as in **100**, there is no need to cancel it, as it is considered to be entirely dependent on the arm gesture. Therefore, in **100**, the forward participation dissolves with the opening movement and the downward participation is valid as long as the downward arm movement.

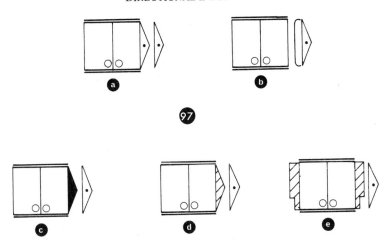

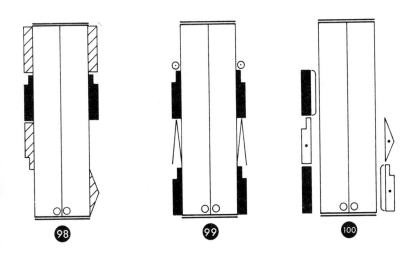

Read **101**, which is a sequence of upper part of the body movements. It is about twisting, rounding, arching, bending and circling. Notice the different cancellation methods used. As nothing is written for the arms, they would simply hang down. If preferred they may be moved to help the body actions, although this would not be a correct reading.

Read **102**. The body movements enhance the lilting quality of the steps, which are in waltz time, particularly in the first two bars. Notice that in the third bar the sideways bend is less than a normal inclination for the deep arm gesture. In the fourth bar the inclusion bracket cancels the previous bend. In the last bar there is a brief bend to the right, and then the body accompanies the lifting arm gestures, ending with a slight arch backwards.

103 is a series of athletic jumps with actions in all four limbs and the body. In the third large jump the limbs contract in. The body is included. Exactly what kind of a bend this will produce in the body is not quite clear, as place for the body is not fully analysed. However, it allows the body to participate in the contraction somehow. Notice that the right arm keeps its position horizontally to the right, although the body leans to the right. The arm is not carried down with the body.

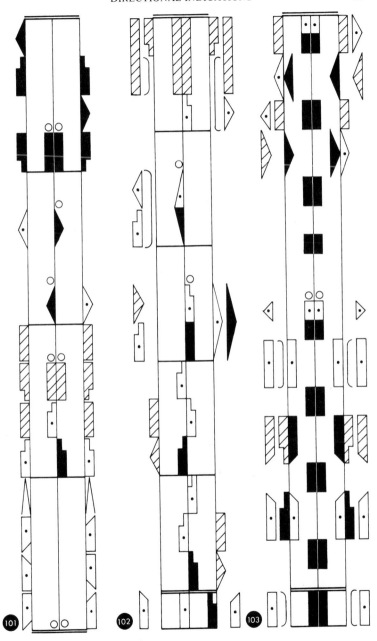

101 102 103

MINOR DIRECTION SIGNS

There are twenty-seven minor direction signs, and they correspond exactly to the major direction signs. Because of their shape, these signs are sometimes called "pin" signs.

104 gives the nine high signs, which are white, the nine medium signs, which are straight, and the nine deep signs, which are black. There are two ways of drawing the vertical directions, and they are shown in **105**. There is no difference in the meaning.

Minor direction signs are used:

1. to show slight directional changes;
2. to make a detour;
3. for the relationship of one leg to another in steps and gestures;
4. for the relationship of arm positions to the centre line of the body;
5. in connection with relation signs;
6. in turn signs and front signs; and
7. in pre-signs.

Points 1–4 are dealt with here; points 5–7 appear elsewhere in the text (*see* **72, 154, 160**).

SLIGHT DIRECTIONAL CHANGES

"Pin" signs are written in an increase sign, meaning gradually move slightly in the stated direction. **106** illustrates this in the simple staff. It means rise very slightly, advance forward very slightly and move left-deep, again very slightly. **107** uses the same method in the full staff to modify a leg gesture and an arm gesture. The amount of movement is quite small.

MAKING A DETOUR

108 shows a movement which, while advancing, makes a slight detour over-high. The pathway will curve out a little upwards.

109 shows an arm gesture, starting backwards-deep and opening sideways, but the path bulges out a little towards backwards-right.

110 shows a leg gesture which has a slight downward and upward curve to the pathway.

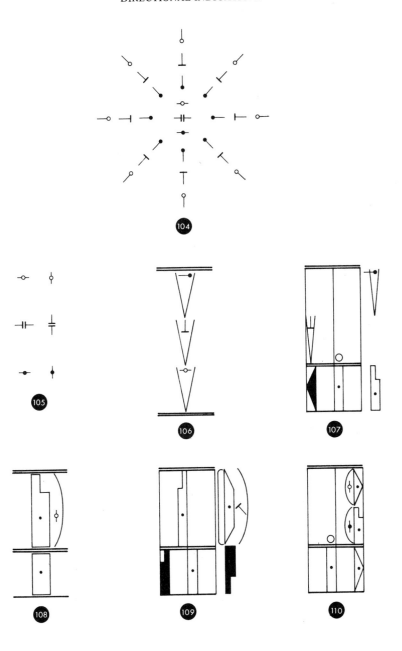

RELATIONSHIP OF ONE LEG TO THE OTHER

Details of the relationship of one leg to the other are shown by pin signs; *see* **111–115**.

> **111** shows walking with the feet one in front of the other, followed by two normal steps.
>
> **112** shows closing the left foot first behind and then in front of the right foot.
>
> **113** shows two jumps in which the feet remain together, but in the first landing the right foot is just in front, and in the second landing it is behind.
>
> **114** gives the pin sign attached to a leg gesture to show that the right foot is at first behind the left leg and then in front of it.
>
> **115a** and **b** show the legs to be diagonally related; the heel of one foot nestles into the arch of the other.

The reader will have noticed that deep pin signs are used here. This is because: (*a*) the level has no significance and therefore any level could be used, and (*b*) the legibility of deep pins is superior to medium or high ones.

Read **116**, which is a sequence of steps and jumps in which the relationship of one leg to the other is indicated.

RELATIONSHIP OF ARM POSITIONS TO THE CENTRE LINE OF THE BODY

When the arm moves forward the hand is in front of the shoulder, but it is sometimes necessary to be able to say that an arm moves so that the hand is directly in front of, or behind, the middle line of the body.

In **117** the pin sign states that the down-ward and forward movements are in line with the centre line of the body. Note that the left arm is downwards and behind the body, and also that the convention of deep pin signs is used. In the ending position the left hand will be directly above the right, both arms being in front of the centre line of the body.

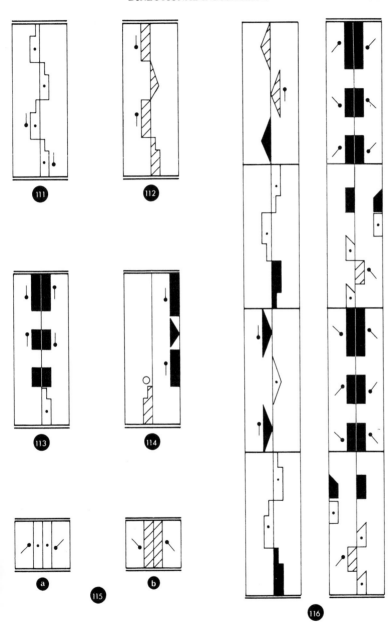

IN-BETWEEN DIRECTIONS

In very detailed kinetograms, where it is necessary to describe the exact direction of actions, the twenty-seven directions commonly used may not be sufficient. The angle between one direction and another is 45°, but, where necessary, this angle can be reduced to 15°. This is done by writing minor directions in to the major direction signs.

118a shows in-between directions. The right half of the diagram shows the directions from high to right to deep, and the left side from high to forwards to deep. The method is to insert the pin sign for the direction towards which the movement is deflected. There are therefore two in-between directions between each major change.

118b shows the eight variants which can be made from the direction horizontally right. There are eight variants of each major direction except for the high and deep diagonal directions, which have six variants.

In **119** in-between directions are shown for arm movements and steps. Note that the deep level pin sign in the left leg's step will mean that the level of the step is just a little lower than usual, which will make the knee bend very slightly.

TOWARDS AND AWAY

Before the subject of direction is finished mention must be made of one other way of describing direction. It is used primarily in the simple staff. The method used is to describe the aim of the action towards or away from some identifiable thing. This may be a person, a part of the body, a place in the room or an object of some kind. Signs for the identifiable things listed are given in later chapters, so that for the purpose of describing the method the letter "P" will be used to represent a partner: *see* **120a–c**.

    a means make an action towards a partner.
    b means make an action away from a partner.
    c means that the right arm gestures towards a partner.

In all three examples the position of the partner is not known, so that the signs may be describing actions in to any actual direction.

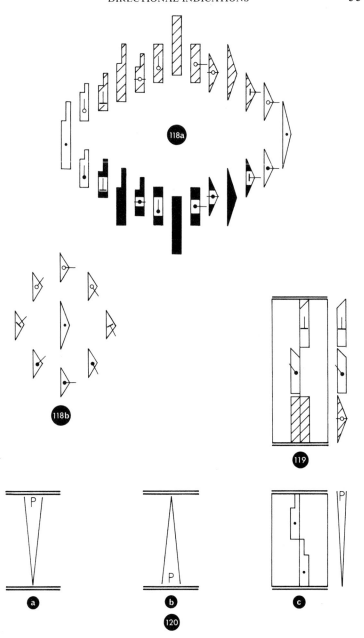

Chapter Three

CONTRACTION, EXTENSION AND SIZE

121a is the basic sign for contracting, and **122a** the basic sign for extending. They are called space measurement signs.

121b and **122b**, the doubled signs, show a greater degree of contraction and extension. The words contraction and extension are inadequate to cover the range of use of these signs. Other words which occur for contraction are bending, curling in, enclosing, decreasing in size, diminishing, small, and for extension are stretching, spreading, enlarging, elongating, big.

IN THE SIMPLE STAFFS

Unlike direction signs, space measurement signs are not able to elongate and shorten themselves according to the duration that the contraction or extension takes. The following methods are used to deal with this.

123a. The sign written in a "V" means that the action of contracting or extending is taking place.

123b. The sign written above an action stroke and connected to it describes the position arrived at in terms of bent or stretched. It describes the aim of the movement and not the nature of the movement, which **123a** does.

124a and **b.** The signs written in a bracket are used to qualify an action or series of actions. The difference between the two is slight, and is one of timing and validity, and will be clarified in the following examples and text.

125. This symbol is used for cancellation, meaning do less of what has been indicated.

Look at **126a**. It describes a sequence starting with three actions, all qualified as being small; the body then extends; then it makes a movement, unqualified in extension; it then moves to arrive very stretched, gives up the stretched position, and contracts markedly.

126b is a sequence about contraction and extension in which the active side of the body is important too.

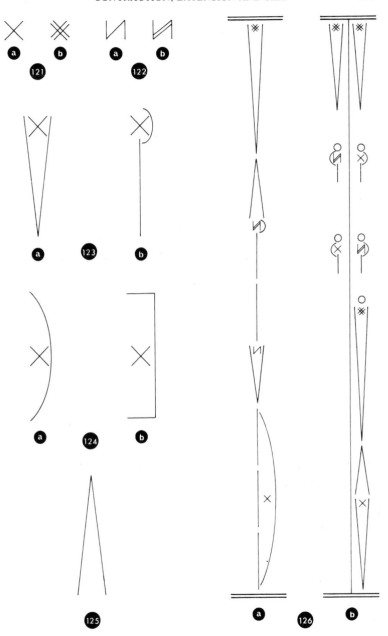

As well as movements of the body being large and small, path-ways can be long or short, *i.e.* qualified as to extent. Look at **127a–e.**

a means travel, or make a pathway.
b means make a short pathway.
c means make a long pathway.

Note that the short and long indications qualify extension, and do not mean a short time or long time is taken, which would, as usual, be shown by the length of the action.

d means make a path which is getting smaller all the time.
e means make a path which is getting larger all the time.

IN THE FULL STAFF

SPACE MEASUREMENT SIGNS FOR SUPPORTS

The path sign is used with the full staff. It is written on the right side of the staff and qualifies the steps taken. **128** means take six steps to make a short path.

Each step may be qualified as to extent, and in this case the space measurement sign is written below each step. **129** shows small steps, very small steps and normal-sized steps, large steps, extra-large steps and normal-sized steps. Note that the duration of the step includes the part of the column used by the space measurement sign. Note also that the indication of size is valid only for the step to which it is attached. It does not have to be cancelled.

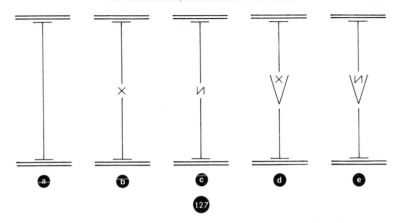

a   b   c   d   e

127

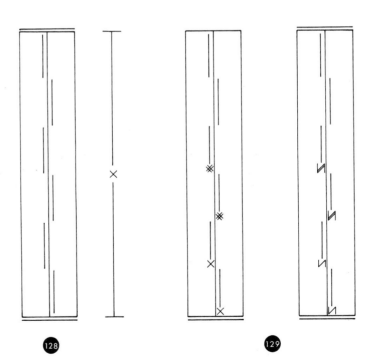

128   129

SPACE MEASUREMENT SIGNS IN THE LEG-GESTURE COLUMN

These signs, shown in **130a–c**, describe the contraction or extension of the leg.

> **a** shows contracted and extended gestures while balancing on one foot and also when hopping.
>
> **b** shows the same actions when the direction of the movement is relevant. This is, of course, only one way in which **a** could be performed.
>
> **c** shows how a half-written score might look when the extensions are clear, but before the directions are clarified. This would be written only as a preliminary to the full writing of **b**.

Note the three stages of contraction in **131**; the leg is at first straight down, then bent up a bit, bent more, then bent entirely. The reader should note that the double contracted sign does not mean bend all the way, but only two-thirds of the way.

It is sometimes less easy to judge the direction of a contracted gesture than one of normal extension. But the rule is simple and solves any difficulties. It is: the direction of any gesture is judged from the point of origin to the farthest part of the limb, which in leg gestures is the foot. The direction taken by the knee does not alter the main direction of the movement: it is the line between the hip and the foot that matters. In **132** note that the very contracted backward direction is quite possible for an unskilled mover, while a similar indication forward-high would be impossible for people who are not supple. In the sideways movement, if the leg is turned out, the knee is much higher in the bent position than in the straight one because of the necessary line between foot and hip.

A word must be said about what extended means in connection with leg gestures. The yardstick is what one considers to be the normal carriage of the leg. Kinetography, as far as possible, always takes normal to be the normal for an untrained body, and in this case a normal leg is regarded as being without a fully stretched knee and with the foot loosely carried and not arched.

In **133** the first leg gesture is normal, the second is with a straight knee and the third with fully stretched knee, ankle and foot. This is the normal carriage for classical dancers, which the kinetographer should note. The extension in space is not very great with leg gestures, and the reader should not be tempted to express the extension by pulling out the hip.

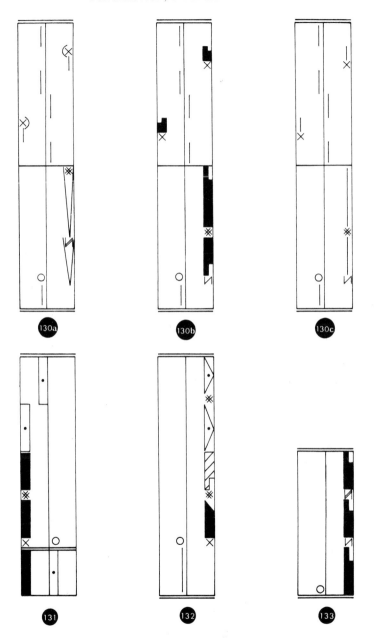

Read **134**, which is a sequence of jumps with leg gestures of a contracted or extended nature.

In bar 1 the left leg is slightly bent during a hop.
In bar 2 the right leg is stretched as it swings across and to the right.
In bar 4 the leg is stretched during the jump and then very bent on the landing.
In bar 5 the right leg is slightly bent.
In bar 6 the left leg has normal extension.
In bar 7 the legs are totally bent up, one after the other.
In bar 8 the right leg stretches backwards.

A contraction sign can be put in the leg-gesture column beside a support. This qualifies the state of the leg while stepping. In **135a** the level is mainly medium, but the knees are slightly bent, so that it will appear somewhat deep. This is often used, particularly in folk dance.

In **135b** the doubled contraction of the legs makes the deep step deeper, and there is a slight knee bend in the high steps. The contraction sign is written beside the middle of the direction signs. This has timing significance which is only really apparent in slow movements, but nevertheless is there and must be explained. As the contraction signs do not have any duration indications with them, the contraction occurs at the moment stated. In **135a** and **b** the steps will therefore have a slightly resilient quality, as the bending occurs in the middle of the movement.

It is possible to be very precise about the timing, as **136** shows. In the first step the bend is immediately at the beginning; in the second it appears at the last moment; in the third it is apparent throughout, and still apparent in the pause; in the fourth it is apparent throughout, but gone by the pause. Note the clear difference in validity of the two brackets: the square one is the description of a "permanent state" and the second one of a "passing state." The difference is needed only when the movement is followed by a pause.

137 illustrates two points, (*a*) that a stretched sign means with straight and therefore rigid legs, and (*b*) that the retention sign above it gives the stretched indication validity until cancelled, in the last two steps, by the usual cancellation method.

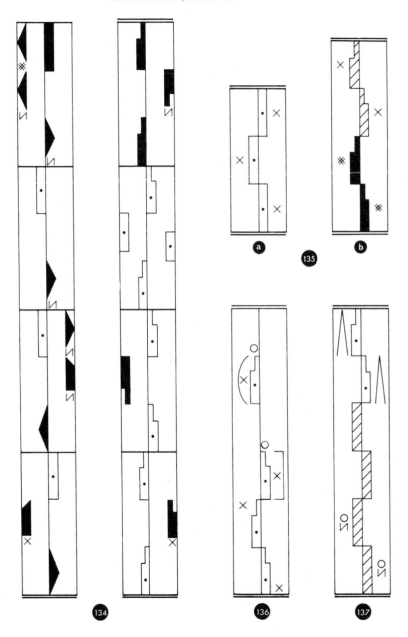

SPACE MEASUREMENT SIGNS IN THE ARM-GESTURE COLUMN

These describe the contraction and extension of the arm. When all that is needed is a statement of arm bending and stretching, or arms arriving at bent and stretched positions, then the same method is used as for leg gestures, as given on the preceding page. When the direction and the contraction or extension are important, then direction signs and space measurement signs are written. The direction of contracted arm gestures is taken from the shoulder to a point in the centre of the palm. The normal carriage of the arm is considered as slightly bent, with the hand somewhat rounded. Extended means that the elbow stretches, very extended, that the elbow and hand stretch, but note that the shoulder is not pulled out into the direction.

Read **138**. The spatial pattern is performed twice, once on the right and once on the left. But in the latter the accompanying arm, the body and the legs are more active. A sequence which has extension changes is much more natural than one without them, as will be immediately felt if this sequence is performed as it is written and then as if it did not contain space measurement signs.

SPACE MEASUREMENT SIGNS IN THE UPPER PART OF THE BODY
  COLUMNS

Only one kind of space measurement sign is used in the upper part of the body columns and that is the extension sign.

139 shows the upper part of the body pulled out towards the stated direction; that side of the body stretches out. In the last movement, the shoulder is lifted up and the whole side stretched.

In **140** the space measurement sign is included in the vertical bracket when the body is stretched out into the same direction as the arm.

There is no need to use contraction signs, as bending the body is shown simply by a direction sign in the third column. However, note **141**, when no direction signs are used, which is when a general statement is wanted, the contraction sign can be used to indicate a bending of some kind, but it is not used with direction signs in this column.

Read **142** on the next page. It is an excerpt from a rhythmical dance study in which contrasts of extension are an ingredient.

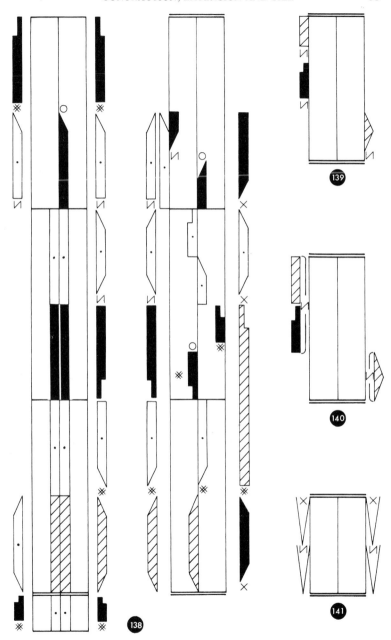

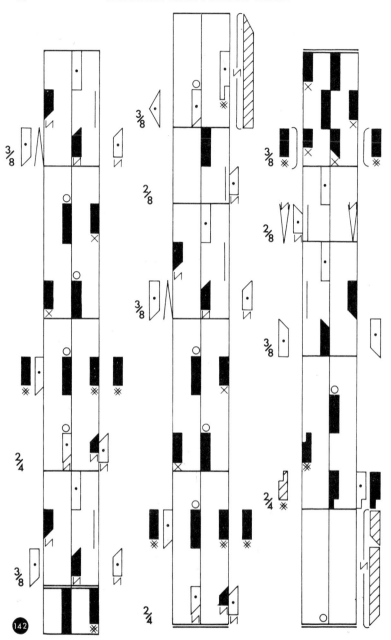

SPECIFIC CONTRACTIONS

Further differentiations are made in contractions and extensions. A line is drawn through the extension sign to indicate expansion in more than one dimension, as in **143**. **144** shows an extension of the body in one dimension, and then a contraction and an expansion of the body in more than one dimension, best described as closing in and spreading out.

The line is also used for contractions to show over which surface the contraction happens: *see* **145a–h**.

    a means contract the front of the body.
    b means contract the back of the body.
    c means contract the right side.
    d means contract the left side.
    e means contract the right-forward surface.
    f means contract the left-forward surface.
    g means contract the left-backward surface.
    h means contract the right-backward surface.

A similar device is used with the extension sign. Hence **146a** means stretch the front of the body, **146b** means stretch the right side and **146c** means stretch over the left surface. The result of this stretching in the simple staff is a "banana-shaped" position of the whole body.

These signs are also used for movements of the hands and the trunk, which are given in Chapter Five.

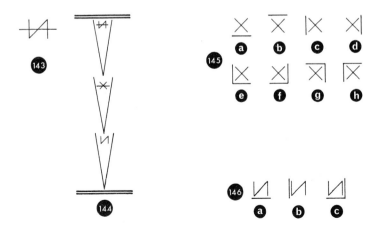

DEGREES

Where necessary, a scale of six degrees can be used with space measurement signs. When this is used with leg and arm gestures it means that the knee or elbow are bent, giving degrees which alter by 30°, and that the distance from the extremity to the origin of the limb is divided into smaller sections. The scale of degrees is shown in **147a–f**.

    a means bent to a 150° angle or five-sixths of the normal distance.

    b means bent to a 120° angle or two-thirds of the normal distance.

    c means bent to a 90° angle or half of the normal distance.

    d means bent to a 60° angle or one-third of the normal distance.

    e means bent to a 30° angle or one-sixth of the normal distance.

    f means totally bent or at the point of origin.

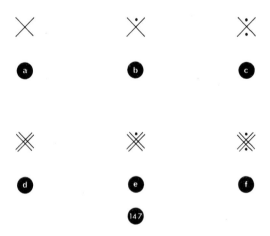

In the simple staff, **a**, **d** and **f** are used almost exclusively and are described as contracting slightly, definitely and completely.

SPACE MEASUREMENT SIGNS WITH OTHER SIGNS

Space measurement signs are also used as follows:

(*a*) With a body sign to show the contraction or extension of a small part of the body (*see* Chapter Five).

(*b*) In a relation sign to show surrounding of some kind during a relationship (*see* Chapter Six).

Chapter Four

TURNING, CIRCLING AND TWISTING

TURNING

TURNING is shown by another kind of elaboration of the action stroke.

148 shows the turn sign; **148a** is for clockwise turns and **148b** for anticlockwise turns. The length of the symbol indicates the duration of the turn.

IN THE SIMPLE STAFFS

149 shows a very quick turn, one of medium duration and a slow one, clockwise, anticlockwise and then clockwise again. What is known about the action in **149**? The whole body turns around its own axis. The rhythm is precise. The amount of turn, the level and number of steps and accompanying gestures are not stated, and are therefore open to the imaginative interpretation of the reader.

When it does not matter which way the turn is to be made the two turn signs are written on top of one another. In **150** there is a turn either way, followed by a turn to the left.

151 is a sequence using basic actions. It is about turning, rising and falling, advancing and retreating. It is open to interpretation, but the reader's imaginative play should be disciplined, in that whatever he does with his body should enhance the stated action. His invention should aim to make the turning memorable to him, but it should not end up as an interesting movement which incidentally turns. Similarly with the other actions.

In **152** turning is combined with other indications. It shows a deep starting position, rising while turning to the right, sinking while turning to the left, and a jump and contraction all turning to the right.

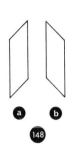

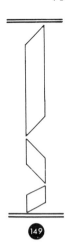

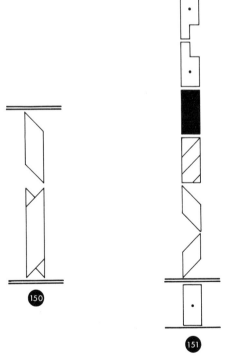

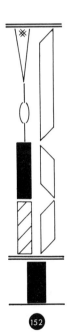

One of the functions of a turn is to establish a new front, and in order to describe this the *amount of the turn* has to be ascertained. This is indicated by placing a pin sign inside the turn sign, which acts like the minute hand of a clock. The pin sign in **153a** is pointing to quarter past the hour, and indicates a quarter turn in a clockwise direction. **153b** shows a half turn, **153c** three-quarters of a turn and **153d** a whole turn. When the turn symbol is an anticlockwise one the reader must remember that the pin also works in an anticlockwise manner. **154** therefore reads: **a**, quarter turn; **b**, half turn; **c**, three-quarters turn; and **d**, whole turn.

Read **155a**. You should find that all the actions are directed towards the same side of the room. Note that the pin signs indicate the degree of the turn, that is, the actual amount of the turn; they do not point to the new front. However, it is helpful to be able to see easily what direction the body is facing after a turn, and this is what the front signs shown in **156** are for.

The straight pin signs in front signs point to the direction that is being faced, the new front. These signs are used in any score that contains turning actions, and one is placed on the right-hand side of the staff just after a turn symbol, thus showing the new front established by the turning action. A front sign is also put below each staff so that the front is established before movement begins. **155b** is a repetition of **155a**, but with the front signs added for further clarity.

If a straight pin sign is written into a turn sign it shows not the degree of the turn but the front which is to be faced by the turn. This is shown in **157**; **a** means turn to face the right side of the room, **b** means face the back, **c** means face the left back corner and **d** means face the front of the room. **155c** is the same sequence as **155a** and **b** but written with straight pin signs to show where the front is.

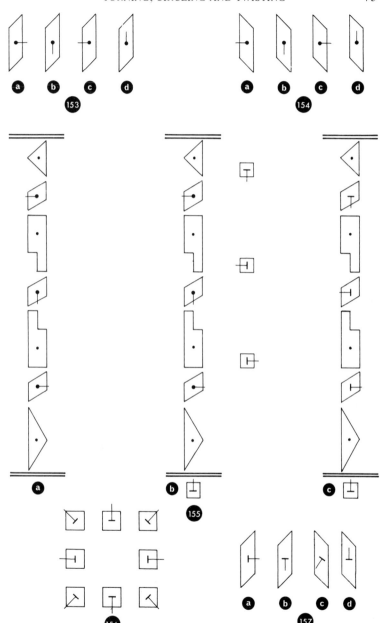

158 is a movement sequence about advancing towards, and retreating away from, the corners of the room. It is also about doing this in a speedy and sustained way. The kinetograms show only directions and turn signs, dead symbols, but it is the job of the reader to find out, as soon as possible, what the movement is about, what the happenings are.

There is a third method of showing the amount of the turn, and this is by relating the turn to a particular point of interest. The sign for a focal point, a large black dot, is shown in **159**. This is placed on the turn symbol, on the front of it to mean turn until the front of the body is to the focal point, on the back of it to mean turn the back to the focal point (**160a** and **b**). It is necessary to state what the focal point is, and this is done at the beginning of the score if it remains constant, and beside the staff wherever it changes. A focal point can be identified as a person, as a place in the room or as an object. "P" often occurs, meaning *partner*, but other ways of indicating people and areas of the room are given in Chapter Seven. Objects are identified by words or drawings.

161 shows a turn to the right, until the partner is on the left; an action to the left, and a turn, either way, to end with the back towards the partner.

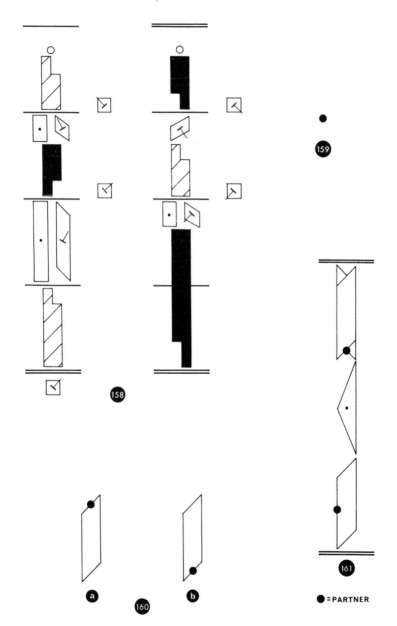

158

159

160

  a   b

161

● = PARTNER

IN THE SUPPORT COLUMNS

A turn sign in the support columns indicates two things, that the body pivots and on which foot it does it.

162 shows a pivot turn to the right on the right foot, one to the left on the left foot, one to the right on both feet and one to the left on the right foot.

163 is a series of steps and pivots. Note that the turn is always preceded by a step on that foot, and this is a thing that the writer must always remember to do, for a turn sign does not also say transfer on to the foot; this has to be said by an action stroke or a direction sign in the support column.

Read **164**. Note that the level of the step which precedes the turn is valid throughout the turning action. If the step is on the balls of the feet so is the turn. This is why it is so necessary to write the step, as it tells the reader the level of the turn.

How do you write a change of level while turning? Look back to **158**. In this sequence the turning action is done while the level of the movement changes. The two symbols are written side by side to show that they happen at the same time. Now when the full staff is used there is immediately a problem as to where to place the two simultaneous actions.

165 is not satisfactory, as it says turn on the left and, at the same time, transfer on the right. Impossible.

166 is impossible, as it says turn on the right while making a leg gesture with that leg!

The solution is shown in **167**. The vertical bracket indicates that the action of turning and lowering happens at the same time.

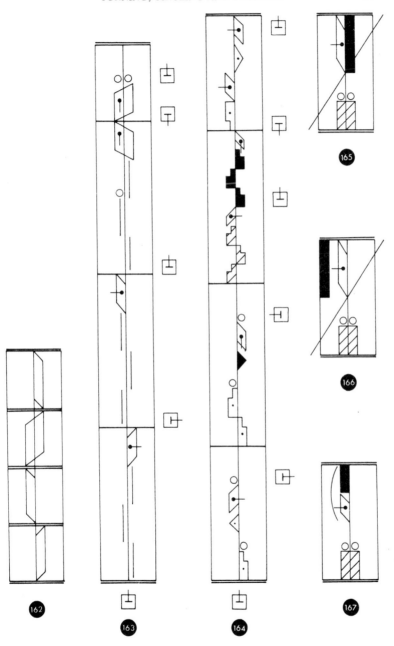

This kind of movement often happens, particularly with rising while turning, which is shown twice in **168**. Notice that in the sixth bar the vertical bracket is not written. This means that the rise takes place completely, and, in this case, quickly before the turn. Notice, too, the amount of turn in this last movement, which is one and a quarter. If the turn is twice around or more numerals are used, as in **169**, which describes three and a half times round.

Try to read **168** so that the lilting rhythm and flow of the action are felt. There is a definite drop down to the sideways step in the third and fifth bars. There is also a gradual increase in the amount of turn each time, which adds to the dynamics of the sequence.

The kinetographer has the option of describing the amount of turn with degree (black pin signs) or with the indication of the front to be faced by the turn (flat pin signs). The resulting movement is the same; it is purely a matter of choice.

Turning while jumping has to be written in a special way, as **170** and **171** show. **170** shows how the placing of a turn sign in the support column during a jump does not have the desired effect, as it cancels the jump by changing it into a pivot. **171a, b** and **c** are possible ways of overcoming this. Notice that the turn sign for a jump is usually placed over both columns. In **171a** the action stroke for a left leg gesture makes it imperative to jump. This stroke can be replaced by a direction sign if the gesture is spatially definite, but, if it is just a gesture as a result of taking off, the action stroke is sufficient.

171b is used when the leg gestures are utterly unimportant; it makes it quite plain that the legs are fully occupied in the combined actions of turning and jumping. This method is rarely used, as most kinetographers prefer to write two action strokes instead (**171c**). However, it will be found in scores of Hungarian origin.

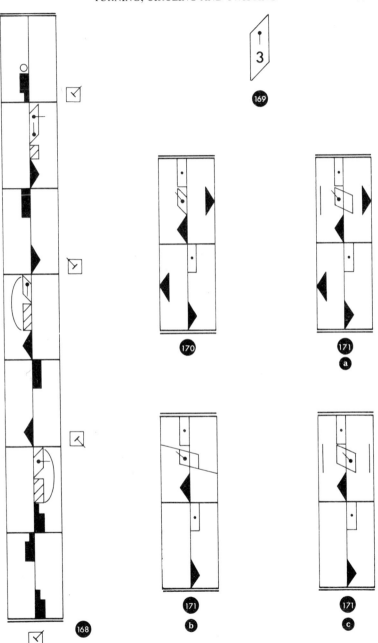

Read 172, which is a sequence of steps and jumps with turns that uses all three methods of showing the amount of the turn. It is meant to be done by three people standing in a triangle. This is not stated, as the method of indicating people and formations is not dealt with until later.

Start facing the front of the room. The amount of the turn in the first to fourth bars is expressed in degrees of turn until the last turn of all. This is shown as turn to face right front. The amount of the turn is seven-eighths, and as this is a difficult amount to imagine, more difficult than a quarter or a half turn, the indication to face a direction is thought to be a better way of expressing it.

In the second bar of the last staff a turn in relation to a focal point is used. No other method would do, as each person has to make a different amount of turn. The turning jump in the last bar is written as a facing direction. No other method is possible to get all three movers to face the front again.

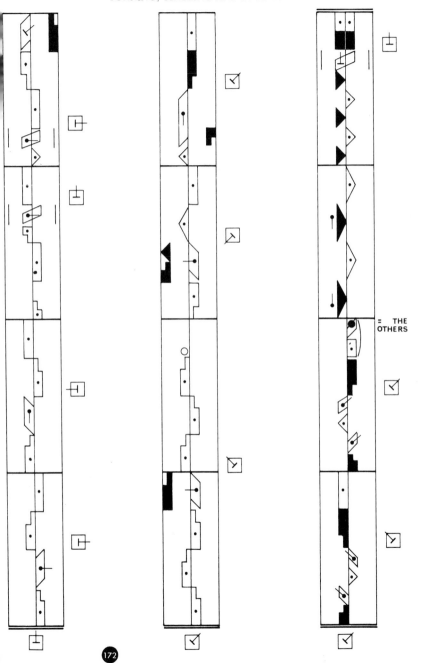

= THE
OTHERS

CIRCULAR PATHWAYS

173a and **b** are signs for a pathway: **a** is a clockwise pathway and **b** an anticlockwise one. They are used when making curved and circular floor patterns.

174 shows, firstly, a choice of circling either clockwise or anti-clockwise, followed by the instruction to circle anticlockwise. Note the way of writing "circling in either direction." The amount of circle made and the step direction are not stated.

175 shows circular pathways being made with forward steps. The first two pathways are of unknown length, but the last two are clearly shown to be quarter circles because of the pin signs inside them. Any circular pathway is related to a centre, and the reader should know where this centre is. Throughout **175** the centre of the pathway alternates between being to the right of the mover and then to the left.

Read **176**. In this example the circular pathway is always in an anticlockwise direction, but the steps made to create this pathway are, firstly, retreating, then to the left, then advancing and, finally, to the right. There are turning movements as transitions between each action which establish a new front and new relationship with the centre of the circle. The direction of the centre has been written in brackets on the right of the staff, but this is done to help the explanation and is not written as a rule.

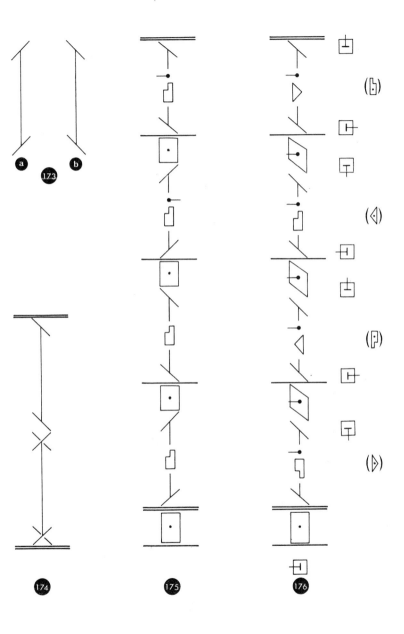

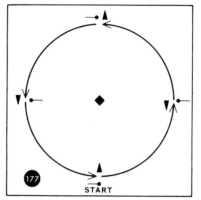

177 shows the floor pattern made by the actions in **176**. The pin signs represent the starting positions and fronts, and the wedges the ending positions and fronts. It is quite easy to remember that in advancing or retreating pathways the centre of the circle is always to your right or to your left, while in sideways pathways the centre is either in front of or behind you.

In order to help the reader know what his relationship to the centre is, there are special front signs which use the focal-point sign to show orientation to a centre instead of to a room. **178** shows those used with clockwise pathways and turns and **179** those with anti-clockwise pathways and turns. Both examples show the focal point as being in front of the mover, to his right, behind him, and to his left. These signs are mostly used when several people relate to the same centre. Each will face a different part of the room but have a common centre relationship, and it is the latter which is written.

180 shows three people facing the centre of a circle. They rise, then make a quarter turn so that their left sides are towards the centre. They travel halfway round the circle and then turn so that all face the front of the room. They then advance.

The focal-point sign is written within a path sign to show that the circle must be around a particular spot or person. Look at **181a** and **b.** In both cases the focal point is identified as being the partner.

> **a** shows A and B circling around each other and turning to face one another.
>
> **b** shows A and B circling around each other but at the same time approaching, so that they spiral in. They then spiral out away from one another the other way. This uses the device described in **120a** and **120b**, that is a "V" sign meaning approach and an inverted "V" sign meaning go away from. General pathways towards and away from a person or a focal point are shown in **192**.

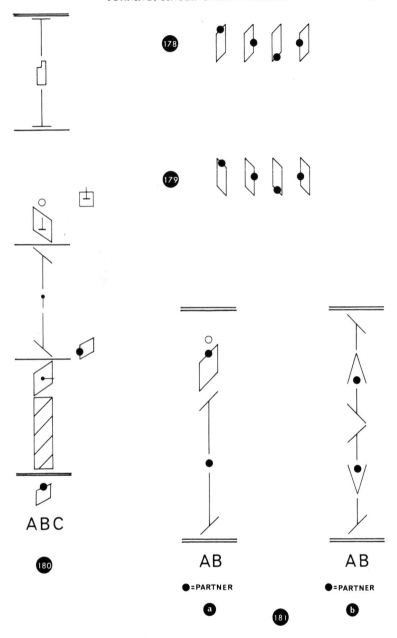

178

179

ABC

180

AB

AB

●=PARTNER

●=PARTNER

a

181

b

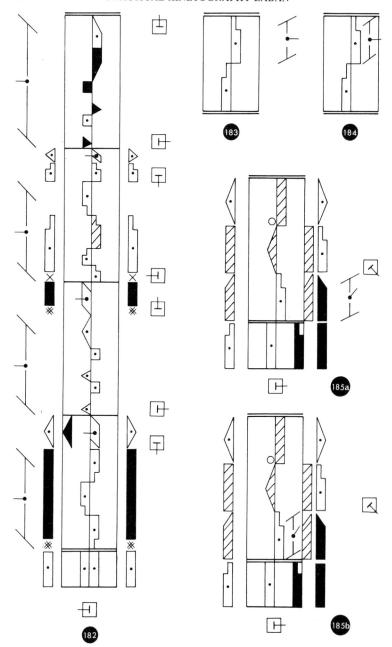

183

184

185a

185b

182

WITH THE FULL STAFF

In **182** the pathways are exactly the same as those used in **176**, but in the full staff the actions made by the body in order to achieve the pathway are shown.

Part of a circular pathway can be made with one step, as in **183**. It is quite permissible in such a case to write the circular path sign within the staff, as in **184**, particularly if there are movements going on in other parts of the body which clutter the staff, so that a pathway written outside the staff might be lost in quick reading.

Compare **185a** and **b** on this point. Both are correct, but **185b** is recommended. The difference between a turn and a circular path over one step is that the former is achieved by swivelling round and the latter by turning the legs in or out without swivelling.

Turning around on the spot with several steps is written in **186**. Although no pathway is made, several steps are taken to achieve the new front, and as in all circular pathways, there is no friction between foot and floor.

A circular path is also used when a change of front is achieved over several jumps on the spot, as in the example of the tarantella step shown in **187**.

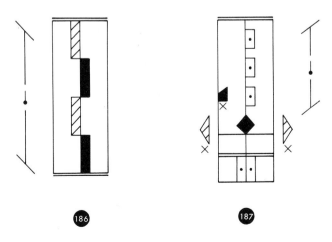

OTHER PATHWAYS

188 shows the sign for a pathway. It is not used in the ordinary way with the full staff because the directions of the steps show the pathways made. In **189** a pathway straight backwards is made, but there is no need to add a path sign.

190 shows travelling in any direction, pausing and travelling again. **191a** shows travelling forwards, to the left and diagonally right-forwards. Note the difference between this and **191b**. In **191a** the direction sign in the path sign describes the floor pattern only, while in **191b** actions of the whole body into the directions are made while travelling. In **191b** the travel does not have to be into the same direction as the body movement, for there is no direction sign within the path sign.

When the direction of the pathway is towards a person it is written as in **192a**. **192b** is a pathway away from a partner represented by P. **192c** gives the destination of the path, in this case meaning arrive at the partner. P can be replaced by other signs if it is not a partner who is approached, for instance, the focal-point sign used in **181**. Other signs are described in Chapter Seven.

Space measurement signs are used within path signs to describe the length of the path. This has already been mentioned in Chapter Three. **193** shows a long pathway made in a relatively brief amount of time, and a short pathway made in a relatively long amount of time.

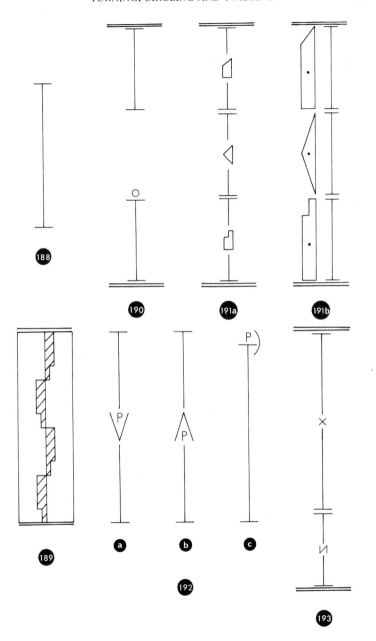

WITH THE FULL STAFF

The pathway sign is used in the full staff to indicate that a path should be made in addition to the actions shown in the staff. In **189**, on the previous page, a pathway straight backwards was illustrated and there was no need to add a pathway sign. If the exact step direction is not known or is unimportant action strokes are written for the steps and the floor pattern is shown by inserting a direction into the pathway sign, as in **194**.

In **195a** a forward and backward step motif is being made, but in addition the person will travel to the right. The travelling is a very secondary thing and is not meant to be a lengthy path; if it were, the

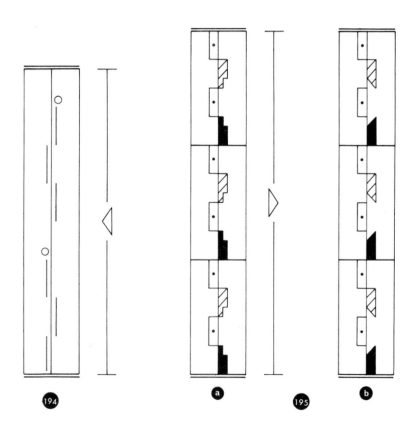

directions of the steps would indicate it, as in **195b**, where diagonal steps are being made. The path sign modifies the action, but does not change its basic character of forward and backward stepping.

TWISTING

IN THE SIMPLE STAFFS

The words "turning" and "twisting" are sometimes confused. Turning means a rotary movement of the entire body. Twisting means a rotary movement where some part does not rotate. In turns the whole body turns the same amount, while in twists the free ends, or possibly only one end, turn a greater degree than the rest of the body. This is represented by inserting a pause sign into a turn sign, signifying that some part holds back and does not turn.

196a shows a twist to the right and then to the left. This may be a trunk twist, and/or inward or outward rotations of the limbs. **196b** shows the sign used for twists either way.

197 shows twisting with the right side of the body, then with the left and then with both sides.

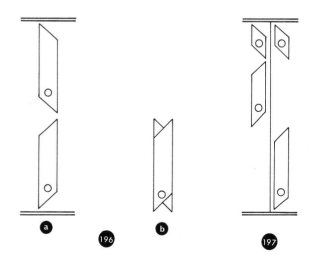

IN THE FULL STAFF

While a turn sign in the support columns means an actual turn of the whole body to face a new front, in all other columns it means a twist of the part of the body stated. The special twist sign needed in the simple staffs is unnecessary.

(a) *A turn sign in the leg-gesture column.* This describes a twisting action of the leg. **198** shows inward and outward twisting actions for the right leg while it is held just off the floor in front of the body.

199 shows how the twist or rotation of the limb is indicated while walking; in this case two steps with the legs turned out and two with them turned in.

200a shows the symbol used to cancel a limb rotation, as a twist indication is valid until cancelled. Should it be necessary—which is unlikely—to indicate twist either way in the full staff, then the "ad lib" sign is inserted into the sign, as shown in **200b**.

In **201** the sideways step is performed with the leg outwardly rotated to increase the opening quality, but the advancing step is not outwardly rotated but done with normal leg rotation.

It is quite unnecessary to analyse the leg rotation, or write it, in the majority of movements. If it were necessary the score would be cluttered with rotation symbols, as the legs are constantly changing their rotation in order to achieve the directions given. But it must be written if the rotation is an essential part of the action.

Classical ballet uses extreme outward rotation of the legs as an integral part of its style; without this action some of its character would be lost. It is therefore obviously essential to write it for this style, and this is usually done at the beginning of the score as a key signature. **202** shows this, and, as the 90° outward rotation is attempted, that amount of twist is included. The amount of a twist is calculated from the untwisted position of the leg, which is when the feet are parallel. Relationship to this position is shown by a white pin sign.

203 shows the key signature for a Croatian folk dance where parallel feet are essential. Parallel feet are also needed for the beginning of a dive, the starting position for which is shown in **204.** **205** shows the starting position of a weight-lifter.

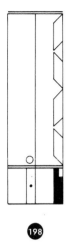

198

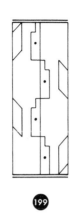

199

b

a

200

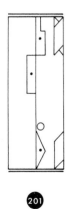

201

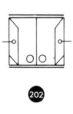

202

203

204

205

It is sometimes difficult to find a place for the rotation sign in the correct column when a new direction and rotation occur in the leg at the same time. A similar difficulty is encountered when a pivot turn and a change of level occur at the same time. It will be remembered that in that case the level change was written after or before the turn indication and linked to it by a vertical bracket to show that the two things happened simultaneously. The same device may be used for leg rotations as shown in **206**.

207 shows another solution which is quite acceptable if there is no movement for the upper part of the body at that moment. However, if the kinetographer is wise he will draw his staff sufficiently wide so that there is room to write the two indications side by side in the leg-gesture column, as in **208**.

(*b*) *A turn sign in the arm-gesture column.* This indicates a twist of the arm, and is shown in **209**. In this example both arms rotate out and then in, while remaining horizontally sideways.

When changes of direction and a twist happen at the same time the twist is usually placed farther out than the directional symbol, as in **210**.

It is tedious and unrewarding to try to identify the degree of an arm twist, because any degree has to be judged from the normal untwisted state, and this is not always easily recognisable, although it has been established by kinetographers. It is very rare, therefore, for a degree to be used in an arm twist. If an amount is really necessary to the meaning of the movement a space measurement sign can be placed within the twist symbol to express less than, or more than, an average twist. This is shown in **211**.

As will be seen in Chapter Five, the arm usually performs a twist because of some other aspect of the gesture, such as the guidance of the movement by a particular part of the arm or hand. In this case the guidance is written and the twist happens because of it. It is also possible to show that the palm is facing a particular direction, and this is another means of showing twists and degrees of twist far preferable to calculating the amount of rotation, which is rarely a thing the mover is thinking about while performing the movement. It also is described in Chapter Five.

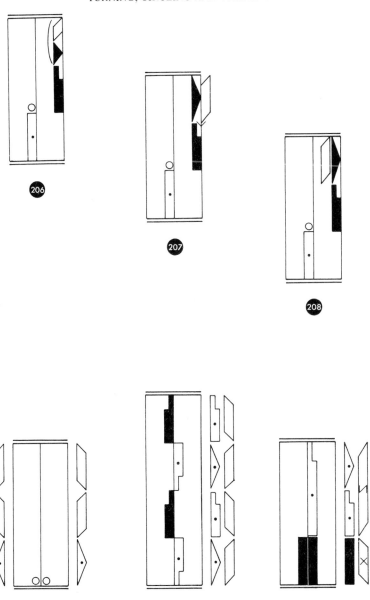

Read **212**. It is an example, in folk-dance style, of twisting actions in the limbs and the upper part of the body. Note the rhythm, which is two bars of 4/4 and one of 2/4, repeated three times.

(*c*) *A turn sign in the third column.* Direction signs show twisting in the upper part of the body, as has been described in Chapter Two. A turn sign in the third column has no agreed meaning. However, one is used in the third column when attached to the chest, pelvis or trunk signs, which are dealt with in Chapter Five.

(*d*) *A turn sign with a body sign.* This is the means of showing twists of smaller parts of the body, and is also fully described in Chapter Five.

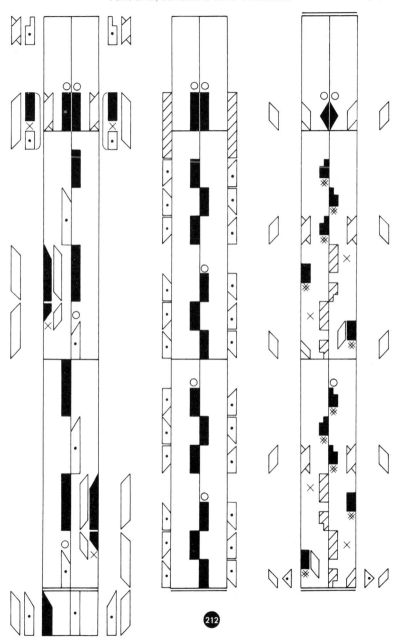

212

Chapter Five

MOVEMENTS WRITTEN WITH BODY SIGNS

213 shows the signs for the main parts and joints of the body. They are the shoulder, elbow, wrist and hand; the hip, knee, ankle and foot; the head, chest, waist area and pelvic girdle.

These signs are used in conjunction with other symbols to show actions and modifications of a detailed nature, as follows:

1. With a vertical bracket to indicate that a part leads or initiates a movement.

2. With a direction sign to indicate that a part inclines into a direction.

3. Within a straightened vertical bracket to indicate that a part is included.

4. With a turn sign to indicate that a part twists.

5. With a space measurement sign to indicate that a part contracts or extends.

6. Within the support column to indicate that a part supports the body.

7. With a relation sign to indicate that parts are related to one another.

Points 1–6 are dealt with in this chapter and point 7 in Chapter Six.

Body signs are used, in the main, to supply further details of a movement which cannot be known by the simple means of direction signs, turn signs, contraction and extension signs, placed within the columns of the full staff. They are used in the simpler staffs when parts of the body play a special part in the action and need to be pointed out to the reader for particular attention.

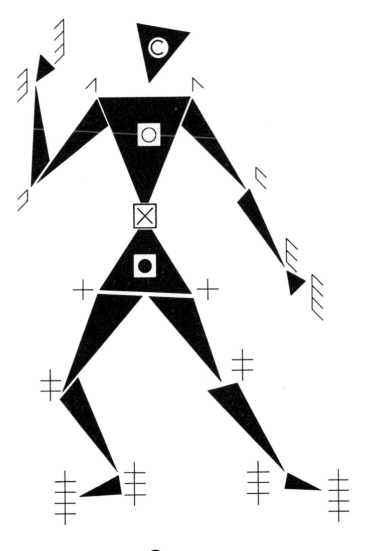

213

LEADING WITH A PART

214 shows a sequence where the parts of the body which lead the movement are important. It is open to a completely free interpretation with regard to the kind of actions made and to the directions used, but it should be disciplined with regard to the leading part and the metre, which is clearly 3/4 time. The actions are led by the right hand, the left hand and both wrists; the right foot, left foot, followed by a pause; the pelvic girdle, the chest, the head; and finally both knees and both elbows. Note that an action stroke is written, meaning any kind of action, modified by the body sign in a bracket, which means lead by the part of the body stated. In the third bar one sustained movement is made and the leadership changes during that movement, while in the first bar three movements are made, each with a different part leading. The last movement of all could be an interesting one, in that four parts of the body are leading; they could all lead into one direction, or the elbow and knee of one side pull against those of the other side to produce a counter-tension; or the knees could lead into kneeling. There are many ways in which this sequence might be performed, and with a group one would hope that each mover would find an interpretation which was meaningful and, in all probability, quite different from everyone else's.

215 shows a sequence which is about turning, travelling, jumping and shrinking, then turning, travelling, jumping and stretching. The elbow leads the turning actions, the hands the travelling actions, the knee the jumping action and the chest initiates the stretching and shrinking part. This makes an interesting movement play with scope for invention while maintaining a framework of clear actions.

216 shows a sequence entirely about shrinking and spreading, the interest lying in which parts are chosen to lead. Note the first spreading action. It is done in four stages, with the elbows and then the hands leading. Note also that the last spreading action is initiated by the whole trunk, which is shown by combining the indications for the chest and the pelvic girdle into one sign.

217 illustrates how parts of the body can be used to lead into actions which have a directional clarity. In this example the leadership starts in the shoulder, passes to the elbow, then to the wrist and finally to the hand. It means that the stated joint precedes the rest of the body.

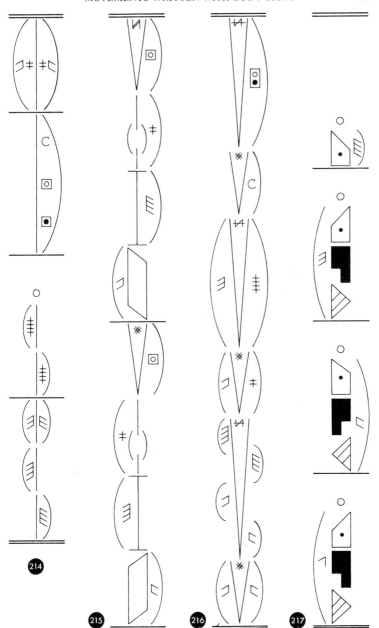

Further differentiation can be given to major parts of the body when detailed articulation is needed. **218** shows the surfaces of the chest, **219** the surfaces of the waist area and **220** those of the pelvic area. Any of these surfaces can lead a movement, although obviously some are more often used than others.

221 shows directional actions in which the leadership is taken by parts of the trunk which are most nearly related to the directions, while **222** shows less usual leaderships which all need definite twisting actions of the body in order to achieve the stated directions.

223a–e show further differentiation of the right hand.

> **a.** The little finger.
> **b.** The ring finger.
> **c.** The middle finger.
> **d.** The first finger.
> **e.** The thumb.

There is a similar device for the toes, but, of course, it is far less used. **223f** is the big toe of the right foot.

The surfaces and edges of the hand and foot are written with the same signs. **224a–e** refers to the right hand and foot.

> **a** is the edge made by the tips of the fingers or the tips of the toes.
> **b** is the palm or sole.
> **c** is the back of the hand or tip of the foot.
> **d** is the thumb side of the hand or big toe side of the foot.
> **e** is the little finger or toe side.

In the full staff it is clear whether the foot or the hand is meant by the positioning of the sign within the columns. However, in the simple staff the signs in **224a–e** are taken to refer to the hands, and if the feet are intended the four strokes belonging to the foot sign are attached as in **224f**, which means the sole of the right foot. **224g–j** are the surfaces of the wrist. **224k** means the tip of the right heel. In the simple staff the three strokes belonging to the ankle sign are attached as in **224i**, which means the inside of the right ankle. When the little toe side of the foot or ankle has to be written in the simple staff it is necessary to attach the strokes to the inside of the sign so that the dot can be clearly visible. Hence **224m**, which refers to the right foot, and **224n**, which is for the left foot.

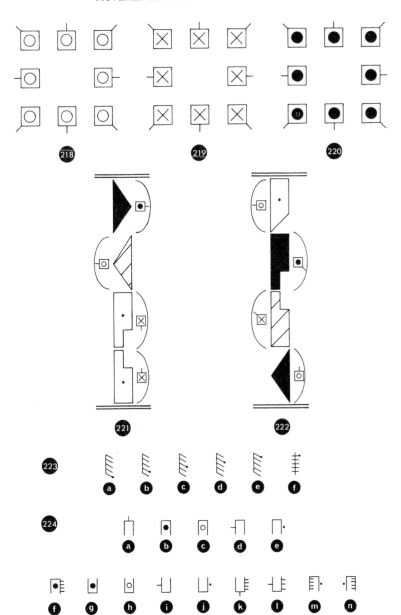

Any joint or surface of the hand can lead a movement of the whole body or simply an arm gesture. In nearly all cases the arm itself has to adjust, by bending a little or twisting, or by joints pulling out of the line of the arm a little, in order to achieve the guidance by the chosen part. The resulting adjustments are not written, but are understood to occur.

The surfaces of the arms and legs are shown with a similar method. **225a–d** show the surfaces of the left arm and leg. **225a**, for example, will therefore mean for the arm the surface from the back of the hand, over the elbow tip to the side of the shoulder as far as is anatomically possible. For the leg it will mean from the top of the foot, over the knee cap to the front of the hip joint. **225b** means the surface from the palm to the armpit, or from the sole to the back of the thigh. **225c** means the surface from the little finger to the tip of the shoulder, or the outside edge of the leg, *i.e.* the little toe side. **225d** is the thumb side, or inner, edge. In the simple staff it is necessary to show whether arm or leg is meant. **225e** and **f** are the arms, **225g** and **h** are the legs; **225i** therefore means a surface of the right leg.

226 is a dance sequence in which various guidances of the arm movements are important. In the first opening movement the whole of the thumb side of the arm leads; the arm has to twist in order to achieve this. In the rising gesture the back of the hand surface of the whole arm leads, and the arm again has to twist in order to lead with as much of that surface as is anatomically possible. The gesture which gathers across is led by the little finger edge of the arm and the turning movement by the palm side; again quite a lot of rotation in the arm is necessary. In the second staff the little finger side of the hand leads, which causes inward rotation of the arm. The back of the wrist then leads, causing a bend in the wrist and lessening of the inward rotation of the arm. For the symmetric movement the elbow bends quite a bit and then extends normally in order to lead, and causes a twist out and in, while in the last bar both arms rotate outwards. Note the transitional step and arm gestures on the last beat of all, which makes it possible to repeat the sequence on the other side.

In **227** the left leg gesture is led by the knee, which bends a little as it leads; the right leg gesture is led by the inside or big toe surface of the leg. The heel takes over on the fourth beat of the next bar, causing a definite outward rotation.

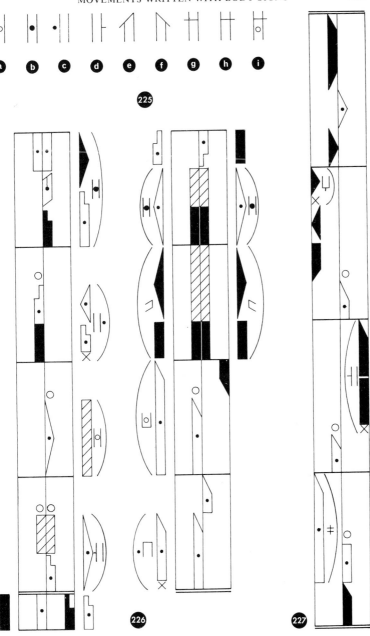

It is most unlikely that in any score so many guidances will occur as have been shown in the examples. The majority of scores have a few special guidances shown, but it is a great mistake, and one made by beginner kinetographers, to pepper all scores with guidances when in fact much of the movement has no out-of-the-ordinary guidance at all. The basic premise is: unless particular meaning or function is attached to a guidance, do not write it. The basic test is: are extra bendings and twists going on which are not expressed in the basic symbols, and, if so, are these best expressed by guidances, or by rotations and by space measurement signs? How to choose in such cases is a skill which the kinetographer gradually acquires. He should bear in mind two questions and attempt to reconcile them in his writing: (a) What is the meaning of the action? (b) What are the kinetographic means available to express the meaning and the action in symbolic form in such a way that both meaning and action can be relived by the reader?

MOVEMENTS OF PARTS OF THE ARM

The basic actions of the parts of the arm are the same as those of the whole arm, namely, reaching out into a direction, twisting, contracting and extending, but not all parts can perform the actions equally well, and some have particular needs for which signs have been devised. In the following explanation each joint sign is taken in turn, and its meaning with a direction sign, a turn sign and a space measurement sign is given, where applicable.

SHOULDER SIGN

When the *shoulder* is written with a direction sign it is understood that the actual movement takes place in the shoulder blades and collar bone. What is written is the resulting position in space. Its normal position is considered to be in "place."

228 shows the right shoulder lifting and returning to normal and the left shoulder moving forward and returning.

229 shows the shoulder leading a forward arm gesture, and then being included in an arm gesture. Included means pulled out into the direction of the arm. The inclusion sign is a straightened vertical bracket broken by the body sign which is to be included.

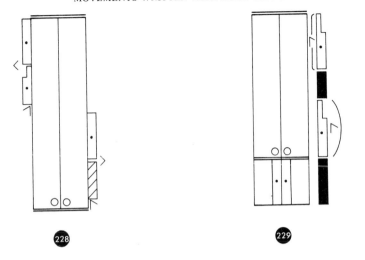

ELBOW SIGN

When the *elbow* is written it describes an action of the upper arm. All directions and levels of elbow movements are judged from the shoulder.

230a shows a series of elbow movements, but **230b** shows how it is more likely to be written. The little angular bracket is used to indicate that the elbow presign continues to apply to the direction signs.

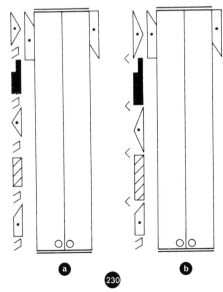

An elbow direction can be cancelled in the ways shown in **231**: by a gesture for the whole arm, with or without space measurement signs, or by a decrease sign.

When the elbow sign is used with a turn sign the whole arm, between shoulder and wrist, twists. In **232** the elbows will lift somewhat and then drop somewhat. Such an indication is cancelled by the symbol for the untwisted state.

In-turning the elbows is an integral part of the arm carriage in the classical ballet style of moving, and is also found in Spanish dance. Apart from these two styles, and in Asian dance movement, the elbow twist is hardly used.

The elbow can contract and also hyper-extend. Both these are indicated by contraction space measurement signs with a line which shows over which surface the contraction takes place.

Normal contraction of the elbow is written as in **233a**, meaning contract over the front of the elbow, and hyper-extension as in **233b**, meaning contract over the back of the elbow. Obviously hyper-extension can be only one degree of bend, but the normal elbow contraction can be in all the degrees, up to maximum.

It is necessary to distinguish further the nature of the bends or contractions of joints. The elbow is between the upper and lower arm, and a bend at the elbow may be made by moving both those parts of the arms or by moving only one of them. When both parts move, the bent condition is described as in **233**, but when only the free end moves a set of modified space measurement signs is used.

234a–e show these signs, which, because of their shape, are commonly called "K" signs.

    a and **b** describe flexing over the front and back of the joint,
    c and **d** flexing over the left and right side of the joint and
    e flexing over the diagonal parts of the joint.

In the case of the elbow only **234a** and **b** can be used, but with mobile joints such as the wrist all the variants are needed.

235 shows a forward arm position; the elbow then bends, both upper and lower arm move. After resuming the ordinary forward position the elbow bends by moving only the lower arm.

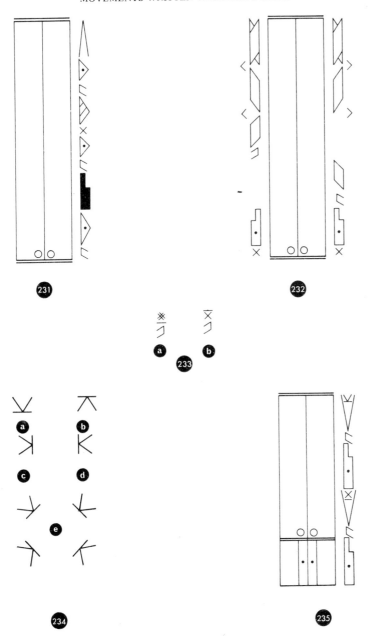

WRIST SIGN

When the *wrist* sign is used the lower arm is moved, and the moving joint is the elbow, from which all directions and levels are judged wherever the elbow happens to be.

Lower arm movements are usually written in the column just outside the arm column, as in **236.** In the starting position, the right lower arm, judged from the elbow which will be near the waist, gives an acute angle at the elbow. The left arm is in a sideways position, with a right angle at the elbow. Indications are valid until cancelled, which may be by a whole arm movement with or without a space measurement sign, or by a decrease sign.

Note that in **237a** the forward indication for the lower arm is valid during the sideways upper arm movement; unless it is cancelled, it must remain horizontally forward. In **237b** it is cancelled and the exact resulting gesture is not clear. The cancellation allows the lower arm to move freely.

In many cases, when an upper arm movement is performed, what happens in the lower arm is that it simply follows. To write a direction sign for it gives the impression that the lower arm movement is as important as the upper. Time and time again the mover is aware of the elbow leading out into space and quite unaware of the lower arm action, except that it "goes with" somehow. A dotted line, as in **238a**, is used to show that the lower arm follows passively. This gives importance to the elbow movement, but the lower arm passivity is open to personal interpretation. A direction can be given for the lower arm, as well as the dotted line, as in **238b**; this lessens the freedom of interpretation.

The lower arm can twist, and this is shown in **239.** The hand is carried along by the twist. Note that the angular bracket needed in **230** is not necessary here, as the lower arm is given a column of its own.

The wrist can contract into eight directions. Both kinds of contraction sign can be used, but the "K" signs occur more often. **240a** shows a circling motion of the hand, described as flexions of the wrist over the front (palm side), right, back and left sides. **240b** shows a 90° flexion of the wrist over the back. The indication is valid until cancelled by a decrease sign.

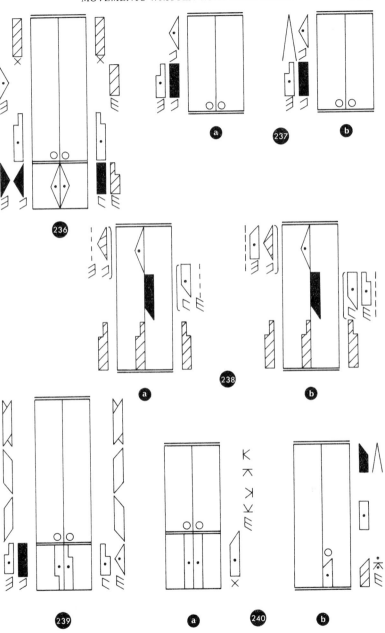

HAND SIGN

The *hand* sign is used to show movements of the whole hand. The signs for the hand are quite often used together with palm surface indications or wrist contractions as shown in **241**. The arm is hanging by the side and slightly bent. The hand points to forward on the first movement. This could be done by contracting the wrist over the thumb side, the palm side or the back of the hand side. An indication for the palm as in **241a** gives what is needed, or a wrist contraction over the back as in **241b** would be equally good.

In order that the kinetographer is clear on when it is necessary to write a palm front for an arm rotation, he has to know what is considered the normal front of the palm in various positions. This has been established and is shown in **242**. The palm front would not be written for these normal carriages of the arm.

243 shows the same movement pattern as **242**, but the carriage of the arm alters during the movement. The arms are doing exactly the same, but the movement for the right is analysed as changes of palm front, while that of the left as inward and outward arm rotations. The writer will choose whichever method he thinks best, but he must be aware that a particular palm front, for example the last one in **243**, can be reached by either an inward or an outward rotation of the arm. This is particularly significant for starting positions.

When the hand follows an arm movement passively it is written with a dotted line, as in **244a**. Similar hand inclinations are made when the surfaces of the wrist lead the arm movement, as in **244b**. The sensation of the two movements is not the same, which gives the kinetographer an option as to the method of expressing the action.

The hand is turned by a lower arm twist (**239**), but it can also twist within itself to a limited degree. When out-turned, **245a**, the little finger side gathers and when in-turned it scatters, **245b**.

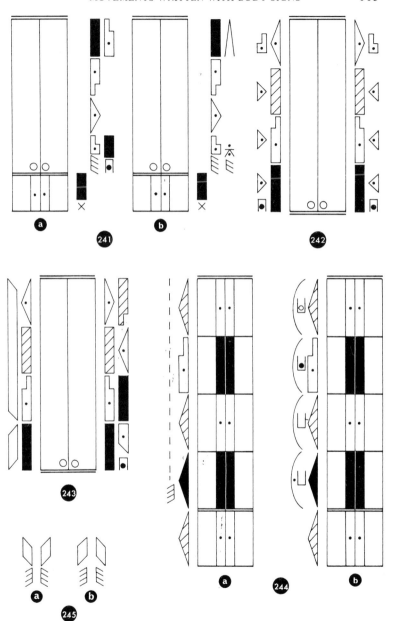

The contraction and extension possibilities of the hand are many. **246a–d** show contractions of the whole hand.

    a is a slightly closed hand.
    b is a fist.
    c is a fist made by contracting only over the front of the hand.
    d is a fist made by contracting the hand in a three-dimensional way. so that the fingers and thumb overlap.

247a–c show extensions of the whole hand.

    a is a stretched and flat hand. fingers together.
    b is an open hand. with fingers spread apart.
    c is an over-stretched hand with the fingers bent backwards; this is written as a contraction over the back.

248a–c show contractions of part of the hand.

    a shows the fingers bent in.
    b shows the thumb bent.
    c shows a fist with the first finger stretched.

All the contracted positions have been described with normal contraction signs. which implies that the parts of the hand and fingers have contracted equally. However. a contraction can be made by curling in. starting at the fingertips. If this were the case "K" signs would be used.

    249a is an ordinary fist made by moving the whole hand.
    249b is a fist made by curling in from the fingertips.

The examples in **250** show positions of the body described by the use of the signs for parts of the arm.

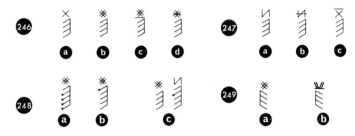

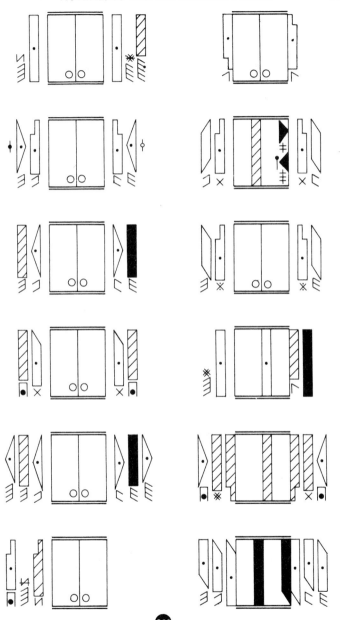

250

MOVEMENTS OF PARTS OF THE LEG

The *hip* sign is used with a direction sign for some movements which happen in the pelvic area, but most of these are written with the pelvis sign (*see* **261**). **251** shows some movements while walking. During the first bar the hips contract over the front and back; in the second bar they lead the step; during the third the hip shifts out to the side; during the fourth the hip is included in the step and therefore swings forward with it; during the fifth the pelvic girdle rotates from right to left. The indications in the second and fourth bars are self-cancelling, but the other hip indications would need to be cancelled by decrease signs if they were not followed by other hip indications as in this example. A turn sign is never written with a hip sign.

The *knee* sign is used with a direction sign to indicate movement of the thigh into a direction. The moving joint is the hip, and level and direction are taken from there.

252 shows some of the typical movements of the knee. During the first bar the knees are rotated in and out; the feet do not swivel, but the twist gives a knock-kneed and then bow-legged action. Note the cancellation sign. During the second bar the knee gestures into a direction while hopping; the indication is automatically cancelled by the next step on that leg. During the third bar the knee leads a whole leg gesture; there will be some contraction and extension in the first gesture and also some outward rotation in the second movement. In the last bar stretched knees are held; there is no natural elasticity, but they are stiff until they release during the decrease signs.

The *ankle* sign is used with a direction sign to show movement of the lower leg. The moving joint is the knee, from which level and direction are taken. In the first gesture of **253** the knee is straight down, but the second time the knee is already diagonally forward so that the position will be different. The next jump produces the same position on the other side. In the symmetric jump the heels will come nearly to the seat. In the left diagonal gesture the ankle is contracted so that the foot will stick up, and in the last three steps the lower leg twists; two steps will be "pigeon-toed" and the last out-turned.

The *foot* sign is used to describe movements of the foot itself. It can be used with a space measurement sign, **254**, to mean that the toes and sole are contracted or spread out; with a direction sign, **255**, to mean a movement of the foot from the ankle into the direction stated; with a turn sign, **256**, to mean the action of rolling the foot in and out from the ankle.

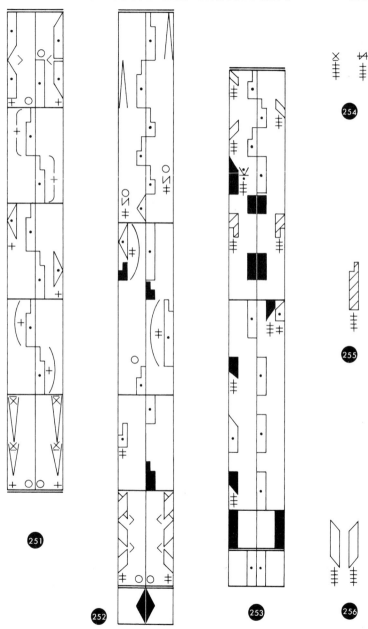

251

252

253

254

255

256

MOVEMENTS OF THE HEAD

The sign for the head is a capital C, taken from the Latin *caput*.

The normal carriage for the head is high. Directions and levels are judged from the base of the skull, and the cervical vertebrae take part as necessary.

In **257** the head tilts into various directions.

There are two methods of showing that the head turns to face a direction. **258a** uses the sign for the front surface of the head, in other words, the face; this surface faces the stated direction. **258b** shows the same movement described as a turn and a tilt. Either method can be used. Tilts of the head always relate to the front of the chest, whether the head is turned or not; **259** illustrates this rule.

Pin signs are written inside the head sign to show parts of the head. A few are shown in **260a–f.**

a means the nose.
b means the left ear.
c means the forehead.
d means both eyes.
e means the mouth.
f means the top of the head.

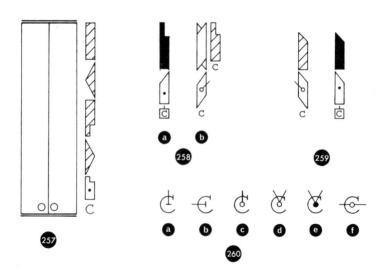

The exact ranges of movements of these parts cannot be fully explored here, but space measurement signs, direction signs and relation signs (*see* Chapter Six) can be used with them as applicable.

MOVEMENTS OF THE TRUNK AND ITS PARTS

The trunk is divided up into parts, the chest, the waist area, the pelvic area. From them the body signs shown in **261a–e** are found.

a shows the chest.
b shows the pelvis.
c shows the pelvis and waist area.
d shows the whole trunk.

For all of these body areas, the fixed point from which direction and level are judged is the lowest point of the part, which for the chest is the waist, and for all the others is the hips. Two more signs are used to complete the ones used for trunk movements; they are **261e**, the pelvis with the fixed point regarded as the waist area and **261f**, the hips. These six, together with upper part of the body movements, which are written with a direction sign in the body column without a body sign (*see* Chapter Two), describe the tilting and twisting abilities of the trunk when used with direction signs, space measurement signs and turn signs.

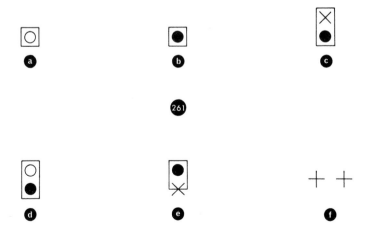

TILTING OR LEANING

Tilting the upper part of the body is shown by a direction sign in the appropriate column. Tilts of other parts of the trunk are shown by a direction sign above the appropriate body sign. These signs are shown in **262a–h.**

a means bend the upper part of the body to the right a little: a bend occurs within the chest.

b means tilt from the waist 45˙ to the right; a bend occurs in the waist area.

c means tilt the pelvis from the hips 45° to the right; a bend occurs in the lower waist area and the chest is passively carried along in an upright position.

d means tilt the pelvis and the waist area 45° to the right; a bend occurs in the upper waist area and the chest is passively carried along in an upright position.

e means tilt the whole trunk 45° to the right, allowing a natural and slight bend to occur in the spine.

f means tilt the whole trunk 45° to the right in one piece; the stretch sign indicates the elongated spine.

g means tilt the pelvis from the waist 45° to the left; the legs have to adjust to allow the lower edge of the pelvis to push out; the bend occurs in the waist area.

h means push the left hip out to the left; a similar movement to **g** results.

The schematic figures give, so far as is possible, the differences in the movements.

263–265 are examples of these signs in tilting actions.

263 shows the chest tilting from the waist.

264 shows the whole trunk leaning over from the hips; note that the legs have to accommodate for tilts in all directions except forwards, because of the pelvis movement.

265 shows movements of the pelvis, judged from the hips and from the waist, and pelvis plus waist area movements in typical situations; the chest remains upright.

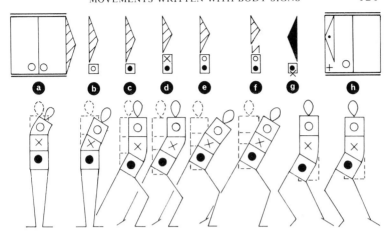

262

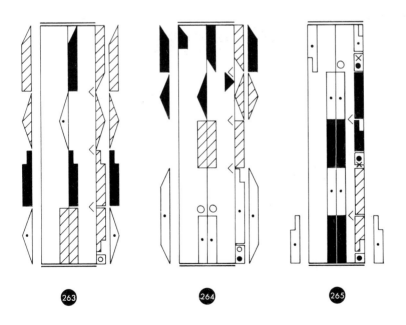

263   264   265

CONTRACTING AND FLEXING

Because of the mobility of the spine, tilts of the trunk are frequently performed with the spine not straight. This necessitates the use of a space measurement sign to express the direction of the contraction. Look at the examples in **266a–f**.

> **a.** The contraction is on the right side as the trunk tilts to the right.
> **b.** The back is contracted, or arched.
> **c.** The back is arched during a forward tilt.
> **d.** The contraction is over the front of the body.
> **e.** The contraction is over the left back part of the trunk.
> **f.** The contraction is over the right front part while leaning left backwards.

In all these examples the direction is the line from the hips to the shoulders, although the actual line of the body is a curved one. The "K" signs are used for trunk movements when a rounded spine results from a bend starting at the top of the spine.

267a and **b** show the signs for the two kinds of bends which occur in the spine; a diagram of the curve made by the trunk in each is given to assist understanding.

> **a.** The curve is continuous and the whole spine bends, as shown in the diagram.
> **b.** The curve starts at the top, as shown in the diagram, and, according to the degree of the flexion sign, more or less of the spine will bend.

268a and **b** show the differences produced by two kinds of bends when used in conjunction with a sideways lean.

> **a.** The basic line of the body is 45° to the right, but the top part of the spine is arched backwards, making the shoulders out of line.
> **b.** The line from the hips to the shoulders is 45° to the right, but the whole back is arched so that the waist area is out of line.

These two ways of describing the bent state of the trunk are frequently used. Together with the tilts of the parts of the trunk, they cover the bending and leaning possibilities of the trunk.

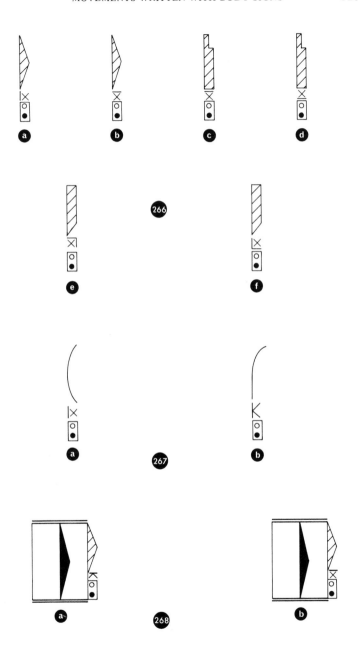

TWISTING

Twists of some parts of the trunk are shown in **269a–e**. In a twist of parts of the trunk one part turns to face another direction. In examples **269a**, **b**, **d** and **e** the degree of twist is one-eighth, and so the twisted part will face the right forward diagonal. In **c** a quarter twist is written.

     a. The twist occurs in vertebrae from the waist upwards, and it is only the shoulder girdle which really achieves the diagonal directions.

     b. The twist occurs in the waist area, the whole front of the chest faces the diagonal.

     c. The twist occurs throughout the trunk and a little in the thighs; only the chest achieves the quarter turn, the pelvis doing about one-eighth of a turn.

     d. The twist occurs in the waist area and the legs; as the pelvis is attached to other body parts both above and below itself, both these attached parts help to create the turn.

     e. The twist occurs in the waist area and the legs, the result being identical to **269d**.

269b and **c** establish a new front for the parts twisted; arm movements following or accompanying such a twist will refer to the front of the chest. The body will have two fronts at the same time; one for the lower half and one for the upper half. This sounds complicated, but in fact it is not, as a real twist gives the mover the feeling of facing a new direction with the chest.

270a and **b** are very nearly the same movement, but note the difference in arm direction because of the turn sign in **a**. The sideways arms are carried round by the twist so that they end sideways from the front of the chest. In **b** the arms also end sideways from the chest front, but are analysed, together with the upper part of the body, as being in a diagonal line in relation to the general front of the whole body. Compare the methods used in each case to cancel the twisting movement.

271 shows a whole trunk twist; the open arm position is held so that the arms are carried round.

272 shows the pelvis turned from side to side while the legs bend; the knees will swing a little from side to side too. When they straighten again the pelvis returns to its normal carriage. **272a** and **b** express exactly the same movement.

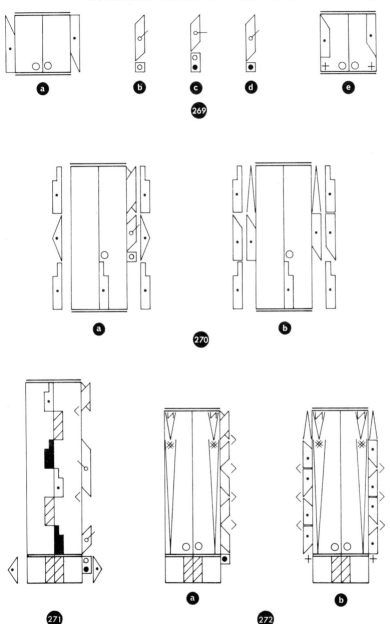

TILTING AND TWISTING

273a–d all describe movements which are a combination of a tilt and a twist; **a** and **b** are practically identical movements, **c** is a tilt and a twist of the whole trunk, and **d** is a lifting and pushing diagonally forward of the left hip.

274a is an example of tilts and twists of the chest; it could equally well be written as in **274b**. At the end of the first movement the chest will be facing deep-right-forward, and at the end of the second, left-forward.

275a is an example of tilts and twists expressed as upper part of the body movements. The last two movements could be written as inclusions of the body, as in **275b**, if exact performance were not imperative.

276 is an example of tilts and twists of the whole trunk. The chest will face high-left-forward after the first movement, forward-deep after the second and right after the third movement: in each case the trunk will be tilting into the direction of the step.

Writing movements of the trunk and its parts is the most difficult part of kinetography. This is not because the signs are difficult but because the movements themselves are very complex, and have great variety. With practice, the kinetographer knows when to use upper part of the body movements and when chest tilts are more appropriate, and to distinguish between the different kinds of bending actions which are made, and to use the most sensible method of describing them.

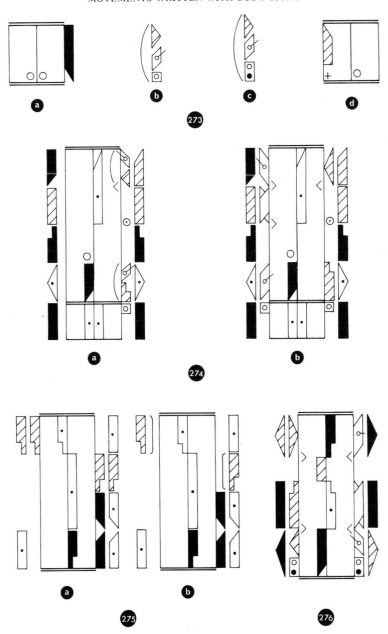

SUPPORTING ON DIFFERENT PARTS OF THE BODY

A body sign written in a support column indicates that the body is supported on that part. Hence in **277**:

>   **a** means sitting;
>   **b** means kneeling;
>   **c** means lying on the back;
>   **d** means on the hands;
>   **e** means on the elbows;
>   **f** means on the head;
>   **g** means on the right knee and the left elbow; and
>   **h** means on the hands and knees.

As there are no columns in the simple staff, a body sign alone cannot mean supporting. Therefore the support sign, which is one of the relation signs described fully in Chapter Six, is used. The support sign is a straightened horizontal bracket, shown in **278**. **279** is a sequence in which the weight is transferred from one part of the body to another. It describes kneeling to sitting on one hip and then the other; lying down and lifting up on to the shoulders; lying on the back and rolling on to the right side and then on to the front.

With the exception of the knees, elbows and hands, all other parts can support only at one level, and this is written as medium level. Kneeling can be high, with the thighs vertical, or deep, which is done by sitting back on the heels, or medium, which is in between the two. Standing on the hands is high when the weight is on the fingers with the palm lifted off the floor, medium when the flat of the hand is on the floor or deep when the elbows are bent. In fact, the level of the support for the hands and the feet is judged similarly. Certain positions of the body are assumed when the support is not the feet. For example:

> **280.** In kneeling, the lower leg is assumed to be on the floor.

> **281.** In lying, the arms, legs and head are assumed to be touching the floor.

> **282.** In sideways sitting the legs are assumed to be to the other side and on the floor unless another indication is given.

> **283.** In an elbow stand the lower arms will be touching the floor.

> **284.** In sitting backwards the legs are in front and on the floor.

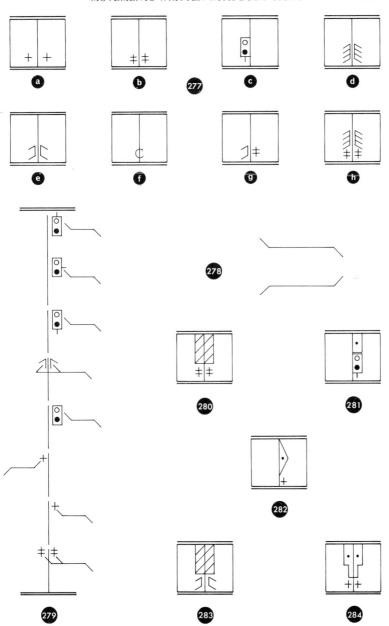

There is a rule which must be learned in order to judge correctly the direction and distance of supports on several parts of the body. It is that, from a position supported on more than one part, the direction is judged from "place," which is a point in the middle of the supporting parts, and that the distance is judged from the farthest point of support, when applicable. This sounds complicated, but is in fact common sense. This rule applies also to steps. In **285** the direction is forwards from "place," the point between the two feet, and the distance of the right step is judged from the farthest point of support, which is the left foot. The right foot therefore steps farther forwards.

In **286** the direction is judged from "place." The jump is directly to the right of the point between the feet, which will finish together; neither foot is farther away from sideways than the other, so the distance is judged from the point in between them.

In **287** the starting position is on hands and knees. The direction forward will be judged from "place," and the distance from the knees. Therefore the movement forward for the hand is written as a large step, while the forward step for the knee is of normal size. The knee will end next to the left hand. In **288** the direction of the hand support will also be taken from "place," and will be to the right of a point in the middle of the three points of support.

There is also a rule which affects the validity of positions of the body where the weight is not taken exclusively by parts of the leg. Such situations are kneeling on all fours or balancing on one hand and one foot, or on shoulders and feet, for example. It is obvious that when one of these parts moves to another place, or another part takes some weight, the other parts do not automatically relinquish their supporting role. This is not so in steps, for when one foot takes the weight the other is released of weight, as in walking. Therefore the rule is that, in these situations the parts are presumed to continue to bear some weight until a gesture is written for them. A retention sign in one of the support columns refers to all the body parts which have been written in that support column, unless a gesture is written for one of the parts.

Look at **287.** At the end the weight will still be on all fours; it does not mean that the weight is released from the right knee and left hand.

In **288** the ending position is again on all fours; it does not mean a fantastic balance on one hand.

289 and **290** show what would have to be written in order to transfer fully on to the parts stated in **287** and **288**, but only an acrobat could perform **290**. If applicable, direction signs would replace the action strokes.

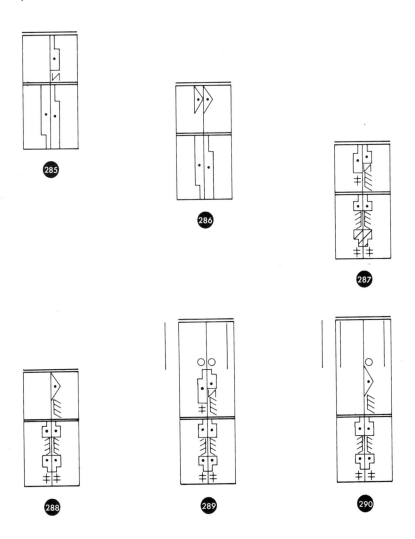

291a–e give additional signs for areas of the body, useful for writing acrobatic movements. The direction of action of these areas is taken from the body part written at the bottom of the sign.

    a. From foot to head.
    b. From knee to head.
    c. From pelvis to head.
    d. From heels to chest.
    e. From pelvis to hands.

Look at **292a–e.**

    a. From a standing position, the whole body, in one line from feet to head, falls forwards on to the hands.
    b. From a kneeling position, the body leans back in one piece from the knees to the chest. As the head is not included, it need not be in line.
    c. From a sitting position, the trunk from pelvis to head leans back in one piece.
    d. From a sideways position with weight on the right hand and hip, the weight is taken well to the left on both feet, so that the body from heels to chest is in one line to the right thigh. Weight will still be on the right hand, but the right hip will no longer be on the floor.
    e. From a kneeling position with the arms up, the trunk and arms lean forward down in one line from the pelvis, until some weight is taken on both hands.

293a–d show body signs used for inverted positions. Again the direction is taken from the body part at the bottom of the sign.

    a. From chest to pelvis.
    b. From head to pelvis.
    c. From right wrist to pelvis.
    d. From chest to knees.

294a–c give examples of three of these signs in use.

    a. From a crouching position, the trunk becomes inverted.
    b. From a position on hands and knees, the feet take some weight so that the body, from wrists to pelvis, is in one line backwards high.
    c. From a lying position, the legs bend and some weight is taken on the feet so that the body is in one line from chest to knees.

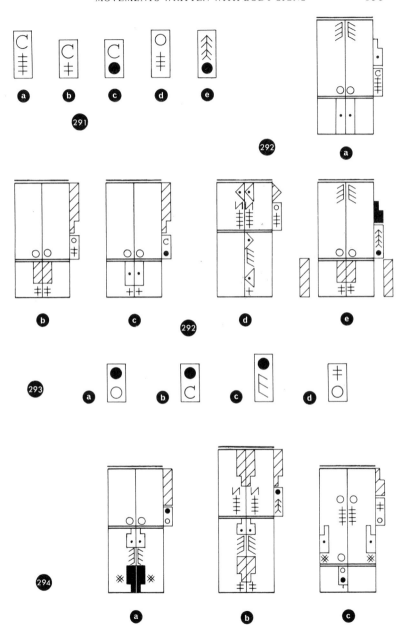

295a–d show transferences of weight into positions with three points of support.

    a. From kneeling, the side of the head and shoulder take some weight forwards.

    b. From a diagonal open position, on both feet, the right hand takes some weight diagonally backwards, the legs bending.

    c. From a diagonal position on the right knee and left foot, the right elbow takes some weight diagonally forwards.

    d. From a position on the right hand and left foot, with the right leg bent up, some weight is taken on the right foot, as it steps diagonally left forward.

AIDS TO WRITING COMPLEX FLOOR WORK

GESTURAL DESCRIPTIONS

When it is difficult to decide the direction into which a new support is made, the motion is described as a gesture, just the body signs for the parts supporting being written in the support columns; **296a–c** illustrate this point.

    a. From a sitting position with weight on the elbows behind, the right leg gestures diagonally open, the left leg pulls up so that the foot is near the hip, the left lower arm gestures horizontally to the left, which will be a swivel on the elbow. The left arm stretches, and the weight is taken by the left hand, the right heel and the left foot. The right elbow retains some weight, but the hips release. Note the release sign.

    b. From a crouching position on fingers and feet, with the left leg out-turned, the right leg pulls through to extend forward as the left knee moves horizontally left. The pelvis moves to vertically below the chest, and the weight is then taken on the right hip or buttock and the left knee, the hands retaining some weight.

    c. From a lying position on the back, the right leg bends, the right arm moves sideways, and the left forearm lifts vertically from the elbow. The weight is then taken by the head, left elbow, right hand and foot, the rest of the body releasing from the floor.

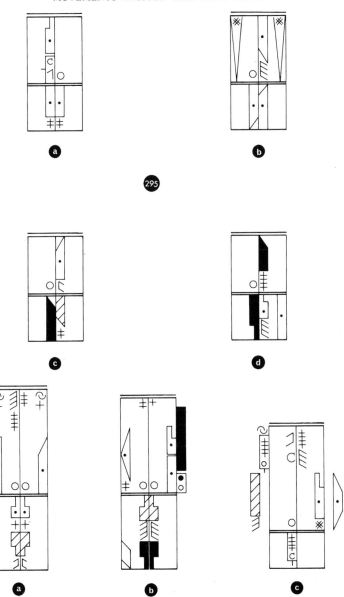

"SECRET" TURNS

The mover's front, *i.e.* the direction in which he is facing, must be known in order to determine the direction of transferences of weight. The directions written must be adhered to even if they cause a twist in the body. Look at **297a–c**.

In each case a twist has occurred, so marked that the mover may feel that a new front has been faced. In **297a** this will be the left side of the room, in **297b** the right side and in **297c** the left side. A special sign is used, called the *secret turn sign*, to show that a new front has been achieved, although no actual turning action, no swivelling, has taken place. **298** shows **297a** with the secret turn included. This sign is a large diamond with a pin in it to indicate the amount of turn, the new front sign being written outside the staff in the usual way. As it is not a movement, but a decision, it is linked to the movement indication which caused the change of front.

KEY SIGNATURES

Key signatures are used to modify a directional indication. There are three key signatures, shown in **299**, and their purpose is to show that a change in the method of analysing direction is to take place.

The sign in **299a** means: up is always towards the ceiling; down is towards the floor; forward is always towards the direction of the mover's front; backward is away from it; right is always to the right of the direction of the mover's front; left is to the left of it.

This is the normal method of judging direction. The significance of it is that forwards always relates to the mover's front wherever the body is facing in the room, and up is always ceilingward, even if the body is lying down or on all fours.

The sign in **299b** means relate all directions to the dimensions of the body. Therefore: up is always headward; down is always footward; forward is in front of the trunk; backward is behind it; right is to the right of the trunk; left is to the left of it. The significance of this is that when the trunk tilts out of the vertical so do the directions, so that even when lying down, up means towards the head.

The sign in **299c** means relate all directions to the dimensions of the room. Therefore: up is towards the ceiling; down is towards the floor; forward is always towards the front of the room; backward is always towards the back of the room; right is always towards the right side of the room; left is always towards the left side of the room. The significance of this is that, wherever the mover is facing, these directions are constant. When facing the back of the room a forward direction would produce a backward action.

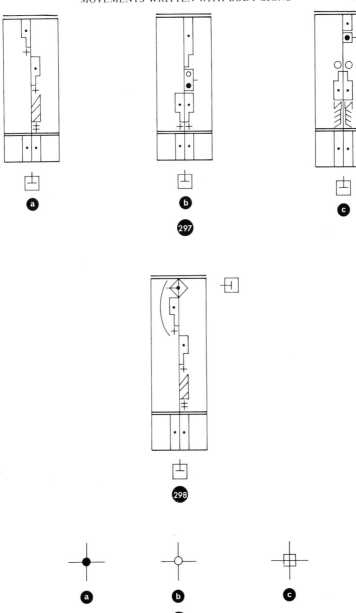

a

b

297

c

298

a

b

299

c

In **300a–c** the identical position would be produced in each key, but this happens only if: (*a*) the body faces the front of the room, and (*b*) the trunk is upright.

In **301a–c** the same action is written in three ways. They are different because the front is the right side of the room and the trunk is tilted.

> **a** reads: face the right side of the room, bend the right knee, tilt the trunk towards your own right, place the left leg to your own left deep and then move the right arm towards your own right deep, and the left arm towards your own left high.
>
> **b** reads: as **301a** in the starting position, and then move the right arm to the right of your trunk, and the left arm to the left of your trunk. The sideways medium directions relate to the dimensions of the trunk.
>
> **c** reads: face the right side of the room, bend the right knee, tilt the trunk towards the back of the room, place the left leg towards the front of the room, deep, and then move the right arm towards the back of the room, deep, and the left arm towards the front of the room, high.

302a–c also show the same movement written in three ways. The differences occur because the mover's front is the back of the room, and because the trunk is horizontal.

> **a.** The leg moves towards the ceiling and then forwards. The arms move sideways high.
>
> **b.** The leg moves to be in front of the trunk and then towards the other foot. The arms move to be diagonally in front of the trunk.
>
> **c.** The leg moves towards the ceiling and then towards the back of the room. The arms move towards the directions of the room.

300, 301 and **302** serve to explain the three key signatures, but are not typical examples of their use. The key signature relating to the dimensions of a room is used primarily in the recording of stage works, particularly for groups, and for sport, when describing the movement in relation to the court or pitch, and it is not relevant to the problems pertaining to supporting on parts of the body. However, the other two key signatures are relevant to this chapter.

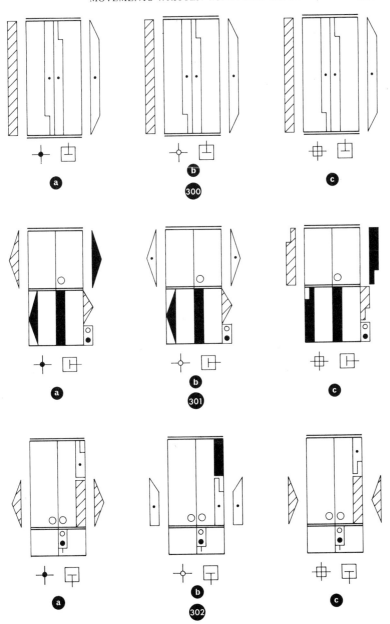

The key signatures may be written:

(a) within a turn sign to show the axis of the rotation (see **304h**);

(b) below the staff to qualify all the directions in that staff (**303a**);

(c) beside the staff to qualify all the subsequent directions in that staff (**303b**);

(d) beside the staff to cancel another kind of key signature (**303c**); or

(e) within one column of the staff to qualify one action of one part of the body (**303d** and **e**).

303a–e give examples of the use of the key signature to aid the reader and to show its placement in relation to the staff.

a. The key signature is needed to show the simple shape of the arm movements while the trunk is bending and twisting.

b. The arm movement is repeated, and throughout the repeat the body, from knee to head, leans backwards. The key shows clearly that the arm movement is repeated, and the analysis of the directions without it would be very complicated.

c. The key for the normal method of directional analysis is used only as a cancellation sign. It is rather like the musical "natural" sign. In music a key with no sharps and flats, *i.e.* C major, is indicated by an absence of key signature at the beginning of a score, and a movement sequence written in the normal directional analysis is also shown by giving no key signature.

d. The key signature is needed because, in the twisted position arrived at by supporting on the right side of the shoulder and head, the normal judgment of direction is difficult, but the dimensions relating to the chest are easily discernible. The right arm's direction is clearer in the normal method, and therefore the key must be written for the left arm only.

e. In inverted positions it is difficult to remember what is forwards and what is backwards, but not difficult to know where the forward and backward of the trunk are. Without this key the leg would be gesturing backwards and the head forwards. Notice that the key to the head is placed between the body sign and the direction sign.

If several movements of only one part of the body are to be analysed from the dimensions of the body the angular bracket can be used to show how long the key is valid. Without the bracket a key within a staff is valid for one direction only.

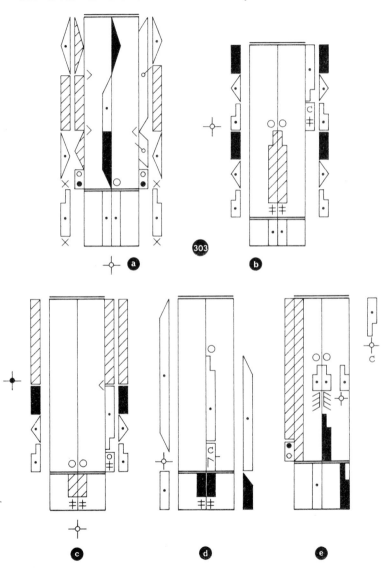

ROTATIONS OF THE WHOLE BODY

The rotation sign so far used in this book has been called the turn sign (*see* Chapter Four). In an upright position the axis of a normal turn is the line head to feet, which coincides with the line ceiling to floor. It is only when the body is inclined that these two axes are seen to be different. In floor work the question then arises as to which of these two axes is to be understood. The rule is that turns are analysed according to the axes of the body and that the signs in **304a** mean "rotate about the axis head to feet." There are two other types of rotation, commonly called the somersault and the cartwheel. **304b** is a rotation forwards around the right/left axis of the body, **304c** being a backward rotation around the same axis. **304d** is a rotation either way around this axis. **304e** is a rotation to the right around the forward/backward axis of the body, **304f** being a rotation to the left around the same axis. **304g** is a rotation either way around this axis. If a rotation around a vertical axis is needed, then the appropriate key signature is inserted into the rotation sign, **304h**.

According to the position of the body, these rotations may or may not produce travelling actions, such as rolls, cartwheels and walk-overs. They may be done as swivels or in flight.

305a–g give examples of the use of these signs in the simple and the full staffs.

a. A backward somersault, passing over the left shoulder to end on the left knee and hand.

b. Rolling around the head/foot axis; the support sign is attached to the ends of the rotation sign to ensure that rolling and not swivelling occurs. This device may be used with any of the rotations to indicate rolling around a particular axis.

c. From sitting, swivelling around a vertical axis until the back is on the floor.

d. From crouching, a forward somersault to end sitting; the hands and hips are linked to the rotation to show the first and last supporting parts.

e. A walkover, with the indication that it travels, as this movement can be done on the spot by people with supple spines.

f. A cartwheel to the right; note the key signature which is relevant to the arms.

g. From a position on the front of the body, and the hands, the right hand being by the right shoulder, the left being backwards, *i.e.* near the hip. The quarter cartwheel produces a swivelling action.

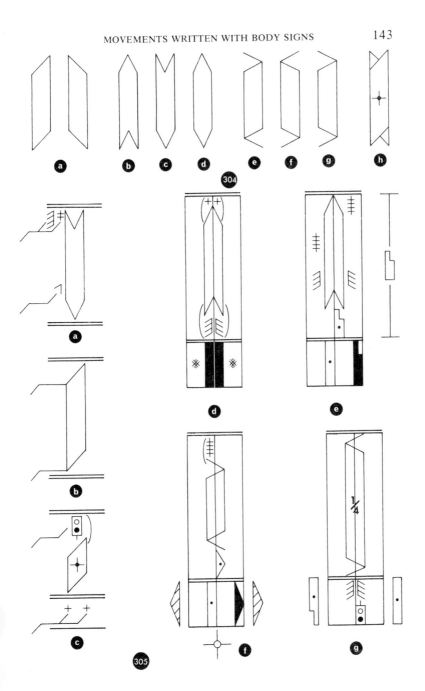

Chapter Six

RELATIONSHIPS

RELATIONSHIP signs are used to show a special relationship between two movers, between parts of the body or between the mover and an outside object of some kind. The signs used are shown in **306–312**.

306 indicates that a relationship exists.
307 describes proximity without actual touch.
308 describes actual touching.
309 describes supporting the weight of, or being supported by, a second party.

If a contraction sign is inserted into the relationship sign it signifies that some kind of surrounding or grasping is happening.

310 is surrounding without touch.
311 is surrounding with touch.
312 is supporting the weight, or being supported, by grasping or surrounding.

RELATING

In **313** the simple staff is used to describe the interaction of two movers. "A" moves to relate to "B," who is still. He holds his position while "B" moves in relation to him. They make an action away from each other, without relationship. If the relationship were to be retained the retention sign would be used. They move simultaneously to address one another, and move again while retaining their relationship. There is no indication of their proximity, so they may be at opposite sides of a room or standing next to one another. Relating may take any form, pointing at, reaching towards, standing over or just looking at. Note that the "cup" of the sign is towards the person *related*, not to the *relating* person.

In **314** someone is looking at a moving ball; his head will move to follow the ball. Note the way of writing the pathway of an object.

315 shows a person "D" whose right arm moves to relate to "E." "D" then turns away and addresses "F." The sign goes either from the part of the body which is relating or across the whole staff if the relationship is general.

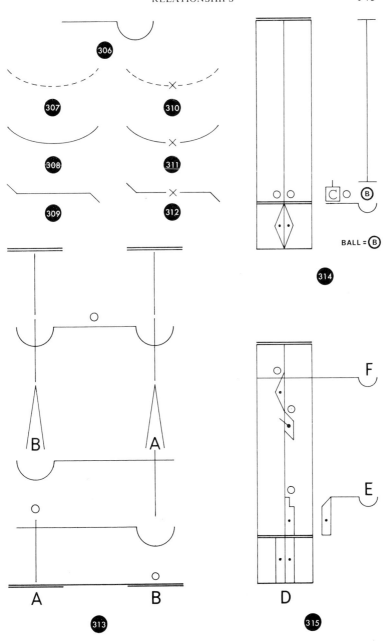

306

307   310

308   311

309   312

313

314

BALL = (B)

315

A   B

B   A

D   E   F

PROXIMITY

316 is an example of the sign for proximity used in the simple staff. It shows the following usage:

> *Bar* 1. When two parts on the same side of the body are near, the link is written entirely on that side.
>
> *Bar* 2. When parts from both sides are near the link crosses the action.
>
> *Bar* 3. Proximity to the floor is written with one end of the link outside the staff.
>
> *All Bars.* The timing of the proximity is shown by the exact placing of the link. In bars 1 and 3 the motion ends near something; in bars 2 and 4 the nearness is during the action and gone by the end. In bar 6 the proximity to the partner made at the end of bar 5 is kept and another part ends near an object.

NOTE: The link may be written curving up or down; there is no difference in meaning.

317 is one possible version of **316** written out fully.

NOTE:

> (i) The use of the T in a square, which means *terra* or floor.
>
> (ii) In the last bar of this example the proximity of the right foot to the partner is cancelled by the step forward. In the simple staff a release sign would have to be written to allow this choice of performance.

SURROUNDING WITHOUT TOUCH

Basically the rules for the previous relationship signs are the same with this sign. What is new is the placing of the X within the link. The X is written at the surrounding party's end of the link. Therefore in **318a** the mover surrounds a focal point, and in **319a** both hands surround.

318b is one way of performing **318a**. Note the use of "towards" in the full staff when the actual direction is not known; this is usually because the focus is: (*a*) moving, or (*b*) in a different place for several performers, or (*c*) in a different place at each performance.

319b shows that in mutual surrounding the X can be written in the middle of the link if space allows.

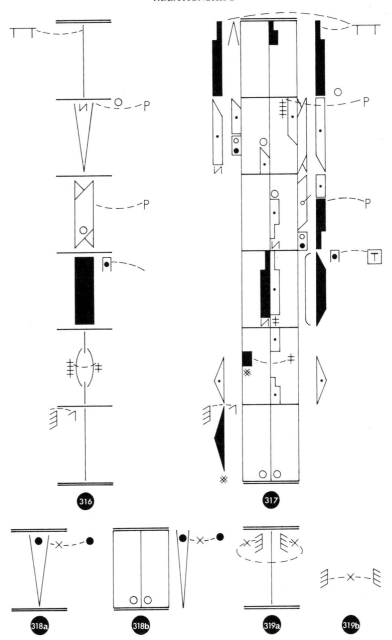

TOUCHING

A solid curved link means touching; the same rules are used as for proximity. In both proximity and touching it is sometimes not clear who is the active relator. If this clarity is necessary one end of the link is thickened.

In **320** "D" touches "E" first; the second touch is presumably mutual, as both are moving. The third touch is made by "D," although both are moving. The last move illustrates an action while keeping the contact made during the action.

321 shows a position with the hand on the waist.

322 shows the legs touching during a jump.

323 shows which hand actively touches.

SURROUNDING WITH TOUCH

An X within a solid curved link means surrounding with touch. This is often synonymous with grasping.

324: the mover grasps his partner's hand;
     both arms surround and touch each other;
     the right hand grasps the left wrist.

325 is a standard ballroom hold.

326 shows the action of sucking one's thumb.

327 shows little fingers grasping each other.

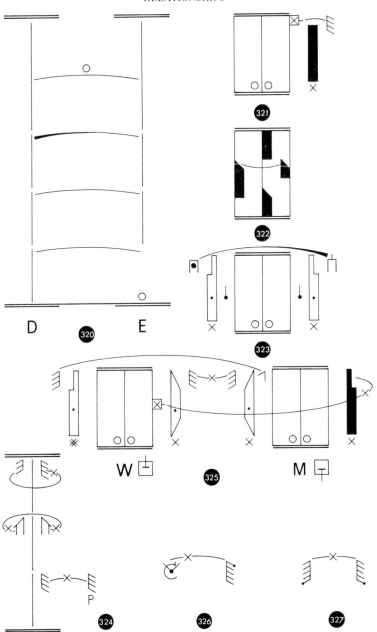

D   E

320

321

322

323

W   M

325

324

326

327

SUPPORTING

A solid straight link means supporting or being supported.

328 shows a sequence which includes supporting on two pieces of apparatus. It reads: travel and jump to support on a "horse," followed by an action to end supported on a mat. The diagrams of the pieces of apparatus are not standardised.

NOTE: The ends of the support link are drawn to be pictorially helpful with regard to what is on what, *i.e.* the body is on the apparatus.

329 illustrates two points:

(*a*) It shows that the support is the floor.
(*b*) It shows the parts of the body that are weight-bearing.

To be supported by the floor is regarded as normal, and therefore the link ends outside the staff and no diagram representing "floor" is necessary. It is used when a support is the important part of the movement, as, of course, the majority of movements are in any case supported by the floor.

329 is a sequence of actions with weight being transferred on to the hips, both hands and the right knee, and then the front of the whole body.

When the support is another person the link goes across to the second staff.

In **330** "B" supports "A" as he jumps, then vice versa; they move towards each other and support partly on each other and partly on the floor.

331–334 show support signs in the full staff. They are much less used in this staff, as a body sign in the support column means what is expressed in **329**. The support link is used only when support is not the floor.

> **331.** This shows a person changing his position from standing up to sitting on a chair.
>
> **332.** A plate, represented in this case by P in a circle, is on the mover's right arm, probably the hand, but not expressly so.
>
> **333.** The body is leaning so that the right shoulder is against a wall (W in a square), with weight on both feet and shoulder.
>
> **334.** This is the way in which floating on water is shown. An A in a square is a standard sign, meaning *aqua*. Note that the support link is drawn across the whole staff. In this instance the mover is floating on his back.

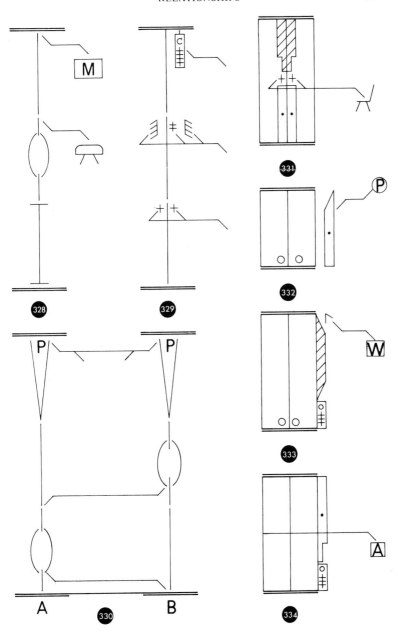

M

328

C

329

P   P

A   B
330

331

P
332

W
333

A
334

SUPPORTING WITH SURROUNDING

An X within a straight link means supporting or supported, including surrounding.

335 is a sequence using a gymnastic bar. This is diagrammatically represented and written beside the mover's staff, as one would write a partner. The sequence reads: jump to support on the bar by holding on with the hands, curl up and surround the bar with both legs, and, while maintaining this, spread the body out.

In **336** "B" jumps on to "A," who does the surrounding.

In **337** "B" jumps on to and surrounds "A."
In the full staff it is clear who is doing the supporting and who is supported because the actions are fully written. Therefore the ends of the link are not significant in this respect but are placed wherever there is most room.

338 is a supported jump. "B" holds "A" 's waist, lifts her, holds her there a moment and puts her down. Note the release sign. It is not strictly necessary but is helpful, as the opening of "B" 's arms must mean a loss of contact.

339a–c show the importance of the placement of the X within the support sign to indicate which person or article produces the surrounding.

> **a.** A basket is held by the handle with the hand.
> **b.** The handle and elbow are interlinked.
> **c.** A hat is on the head, *i.e.* around it.

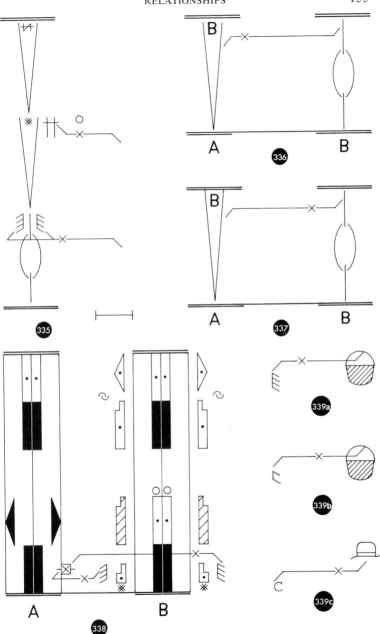

335

336

337

338

A   B

339a

339b

339c

BRUSHING AND SLIDING RELATIONSHIPS

Any of the relationship signs may be doubled to mean that the contact is a moving one. This is most easily described with touching relationships, for here there must be friction between the two touching parts or parties. In non-touching relationships there is obviously no actual friction, but the same idea pertains.

In **340** the palms brush each other as they pass.

In **341** the right hand, without actual touch, slides up the left arm. The retention sign is needed to show that the contact is maintained and is not of a brushing nature.

In **342** a fireman ("F") jumps on to, and slides down, a pole ("P"), landing on the floor.

DIRECTION OF RELATIONSHIPS

Pin signs are used with relationship signs to show the direction from which a relationship is established.

343. "A" jumps over "B"; he relates from above. Note the way of writing the cup part of the symbol, to help the reader.

344. The hands are near each other, the left being above the right. Both hands have a pin sign, as both create the relationship.

345a and **b** show two alternative methods of describing a relationship in some detail.

> **a** shows "A" touching, from in front, the right shoulder of "B." The pin sign relates to the "toucher's" front.
> **b** is another way in which the same facts could be expressed. This way is clearer for the reader, and should be used whenever possible.

346 shows the detail necessary for exact description of handling objects. In this case the object is a cube; the thumb holds it from behind, the first finger from above, and the three others from in front. The palm is close to it from the right. As the cube has no identifiable front, pin signs must be used.

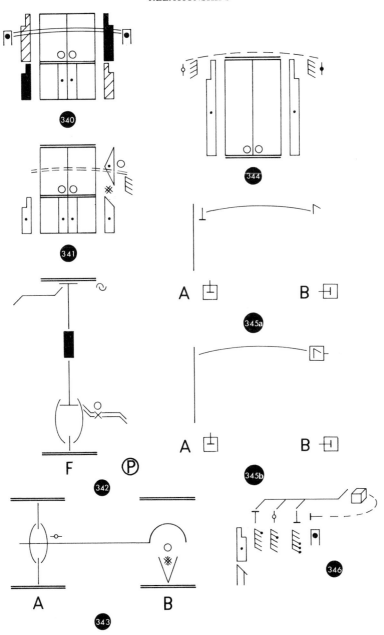

340

341

342

F   Ⓟ

343

A   B

344

345a

A   B

345b

A   B

346

CONTACT WITH THE FLOOR

In the simple staff, relationship to the floor is shown by ending the link well outside the staff (as already explained in **316**). In the full staff, the floor may be identified as T in a square (**317**) or may be represented by a support column.

In **347** the right hand touches the floor after a forward trunk bend, *i.e.* the link goes from the hand to a support column.

The feet touch the floor frequently in leg gestures. In order to distinguish which part of the foot is touching, the touch sign is varied. It is curved upwards, as in **348**, to show that the toe touches, curved downwards, as in **349**, to show that the heel touches, and both up and down, as in **350**, to show that the whole sole of the foot touches.

351 shows touching with the ball of the foot; in this case the touch sign is drawn straight. Because a touch is instantaneous, the exact placing of it on the gesture is significant.

352a–c illustrate this.

> **a**: the touch occurs at the beginning of the gesture, and there-fore happens while the leg is still almost in front.
> **b**: it occurs halfway through.
> **c**: it occurs at the very end when the leg will already be com-pletely sideways.

Only in **c** will the toe be touching the floor during the pause.

It is sometimes necessary to write that the foot touches the floor without giving a direction sign for the gesture, and in this case the touch sign is attached to the outer line of the staff.

In both of the next two examples, **353a** and **b**, it would be in-correct to give a direction sign to the leg gesture, as this would mean that a step and a gesture were occurring simultaneously, which can only be done by a half-jumping movement.

> **a.** The right leg gesture automatically arises because of the transfer of weight on to the left. The toes keep contact with the floor. Hence no direction sign, only a touch sign.
> **b.** The body sways from side to side, but neither foot is released from the floor.

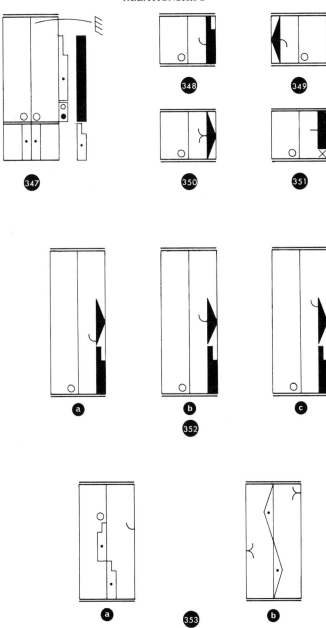

347

348

349

350

351

a   b   c

352

a   353   b

Brushing and sliding over the floor are shown by attaching two touch signs to one direction sign, the timing of the contact being shown by the placing of the two brackets on the direction symbols.

Read **354–356**.

> **354.** The foot brushes the floor as it passes through the closed position and finishes off the floor.
> **355.** The foot finishes on the floor after sliding round in a half circle.
> **356.** A sliding movement is illustrated which starts with the sole of the foot and ends with the toe.

The touch signs for the parts of the foot may also be attached to steps. This is a useful convention.

In **357** the starting position is on the tips of the toes, as used in ballet; the steps are made on the heels, on the balls of the feet and then on the balls and toes. When on the balls only, the heels are hardly lifted off the floor, but, when on the balls and the toes, the heels are lifted well off, so that the weight is pushed well forward and the foot has to arch considerably. The little bracket can be attached anywhere on the symbol, as it qualifies the whole step from start to finish.

Note the differences in the steps in **358**. The first two are not sliding, as may be expected, but are rolling the foot from heel to whole foot during the step. The third is a sliding step.

The rule is quite clear: on a leg gesture two touches of the *same* or *different* kind describe a sliding action; on a support, two touches of the *same* kind describe a sliding step, while two *different* kinds describe rolling the foot while stepping.

The little brackets representing the parts of the feet can be written in the support columns attached to the centre line without a direction symbol.

359 and **360** are methods of travelling along without lifting the feet entirely from the floor. They are found in folk-dance forms.

> **359:** the weight goes from the heels to the balls of the feet while the legs turn in and out in a parallel manner.
> **360:** the weight is on the heel of one foot and the ball of the other, alternately, and the legs rotate inwards and outwards together.

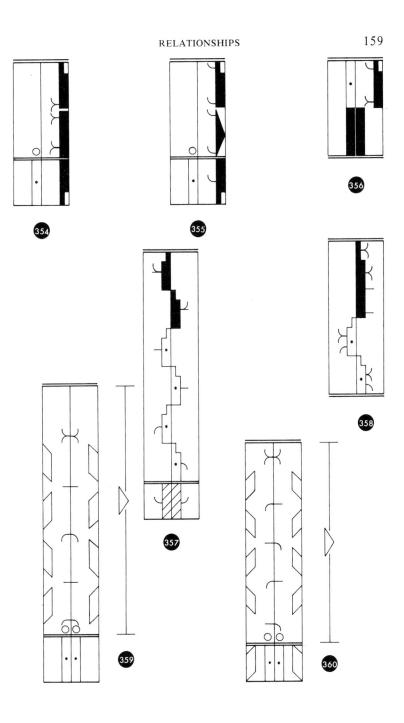

Chapter Seven

SCORE MAKING

PRESIGNS AND THEIR USE DURING A SCORE

In order to write a full score, certain presigns are used, the most important of which will be given here.

IDENTIFICATION OF PEOPLE AND OBJECTS

The mover, or movers, have to be named. This can be done by writing the full name of the person underneath the staff, as in **361**, but it is more usual to put an initial and, on the first page, to state what the initial stands for, as in **362**.

The standard ways of indicating men and women, and of showing how many people are moving, are shown in **363a–i**.

    a means a man.
    b means a woman.
    c means a person whose sex is irrelevant, or an object.
    d means a pair.
    e means four pairs.
    f means the fourth pair.
    g means each person or object.
    h means a group of twenty-six people.
    i means a group of any number of people.

Any sign or diagram may be used to differentiate one mover from another, provided that these are identified at the beginning of the score. This includes objects, pieces of apparatus, tools, props, etc., and the identification of focal points. **364** illustrates this.

These signs are put below the relevant staff right through the score. In **365** "each couple" is written below the staff, so that the man and woman move identically; but after two bars they begin to move differently. A second staff is added and named "each woman."

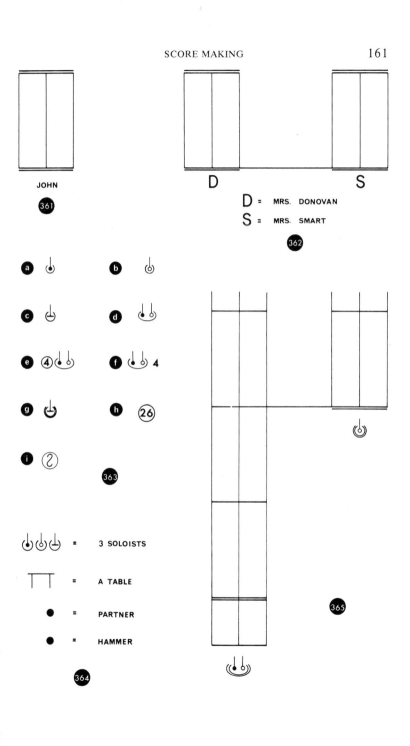

JOHN

361

D   S

D = MRS. DONOVAN
S = MRS. SMART

362

a

b

c

d

e ④

f 4

g

h ㉖

i ②

363

= 3 SOLOISTS

= A TABLE

● = PARTNER

● = HAMMER

364

365

FRONT SIGNS

The mover's starting front is always shown by placing a front sign (*see* **156**) below the staff. In **366** a man starts facing to the right. In **367** the man faces forwards, the woman backwards. In **368** a group of eight people face the focal point, which is identified as a partner. They will therefore arrange themselves in pairs, as they wish, facing their partner.

Front signs may be used as destinations of pathways. In **369** the clockwise pathway ends when the mover faces forwards.

Front signs also may identify a person. In **370** the person facing front leads the pathway.

AREA SIGNS

The area in the room in which the mover starts is stated. **371** shows the basic area symbols, and **372** shows starting in the backward right corner, facing forward left. Further differentiation of areas is shown by adding space measurement signs. **373** shows four areas, centre, between centre and forward right, forward right, and beyond forward right. The latter would be called off-stage in theatre work, off the work area in industrial situations, out of play in sport. In **374** four people are in the wings, while a solo figure is between back stage centre and centre stage.

When the distance from the centre of the working space is known, but not the area in that space, then the signs in **375** are used. They mean: at the centre; near the centre; at the edges; and beyond the edges.

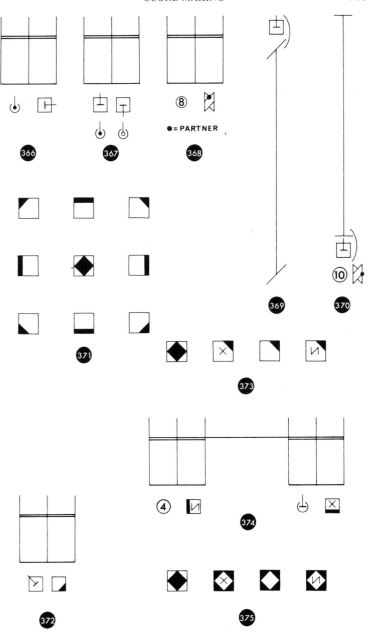

● = PARTNER

366 367 368 369 370 371 373 374 372 375

When the area is immaterial, or not known, the sign shown in **376** is used. It means an area. It is rarely used, but the signs in **377** derived from it are often used. They combine this sign with little strokes indicating which part of the area is being referred to (*see* also surfaces of body areas in Chapter Five).

In **378** the position of working parts of a manufacturing bench are identified. In **379** each trio is arranged, somewhere in the room, so that one is in the front, one in the left-back and one in the right part of their own area.

The method of showing detail described in **377** is applied to the basic area signs of **371**, to make eighty-one detailed area signs, *i.e.* nine basic areas each divided into nine parts.

380 shows the subdivision of the right area of work space, with the details of the adjoining areas. They are used when exact positions of individuals are required, or for massed group work such as rallies, military demonstrations and large film sets.

Possible uses of area signs are shown in **381–384**.

381. As a destination.
382. As a directional indication for a pathway.
383. For identification of a leader.
384. For identification of a focal point.

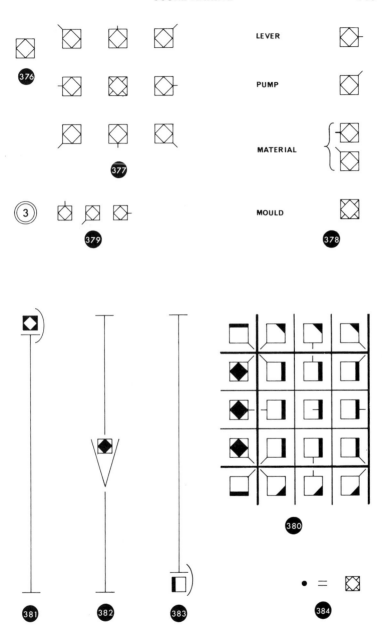

TIME INDICATIONS

Bar numbers are written at the beginning of each new score line, and on the left of the score line wherever necessary to aid the reader. Bar numbers may be written in a diamond to distinguish them from other numbers which occur in the score. If not in a diamond, then any number standing alone is a bar number.

In **385** the group called "B" is in the centre of the room facing diagonally forward right, and it is the twenty-first bar of the work.

In **386** the pathway ends in the area that was occupied at bar 106.

In any kinetographic work of research level, bar numbering is not a sufficient timing device. In these cases evenly spaced numbers are written alongside on a time line, the space between each number representing a unit of time. The unit is then identified in relevant terms. As examples, 1 unit is 0·5 seconds, 1 unit = 50 frames of film moving at 0·0126 of a second per frame, 1 unit = heart-beat, 1 unit = 4 metronome ticks at 108. In **387** the timing is taken from an analysis of a jump, using a specto analyser, and the numbers refer to the frames of the film. The bar lines refer to the phrasing of the movement.

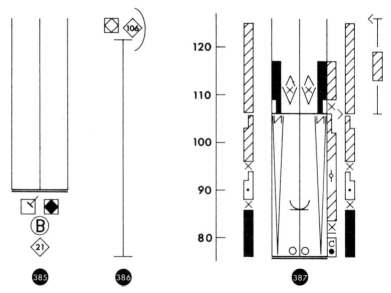

Double black diagonal strokes are written to show where the next score line starts when more than one staff is in use simultaneously.

388 shows a layout of staffs for one page making the best use of the available space.

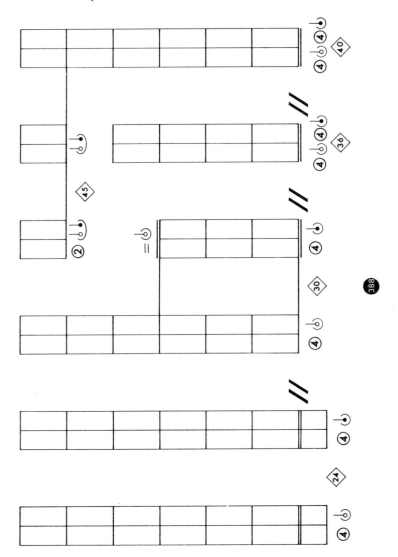

REPETITION AND ANALOGY SIGNS

When a sequence of movements or a whole section of a score is to be repeated, special repeat signs are used.

389 means repeat these bars once.
390 means repeat these bars so that four performances in all are made.
391 means repeat these bars on the other side.
392 means repeat these bars four times in all, on alternate sides.

It frequently happens that the very last movement of a repeated sequence is different, in that it is preparing for the next sequence. In this case the relevant bit is written out and identified by a number, as in **393**. A thick black line is used to make sure that one bar is substituted for the other and that both are not performed in succession.

It should be remembered that everything written within the repetition signs is repeated, including pathways, but sometimes a pathway is to be made, while a foot pattern is repeated several times. In this case the path sign is written outside the repetition signs, as in **394**, to mean make one circular path while performing the step pattern eight times in all, on alternate sides.

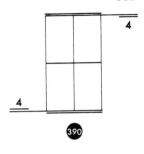

389

390

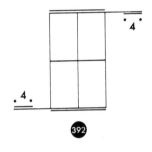

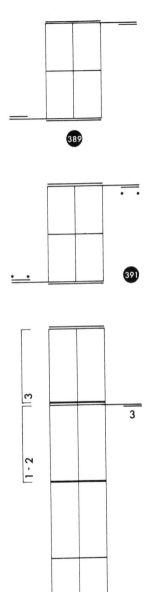

391

392

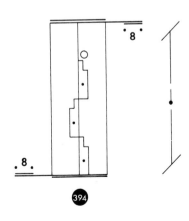

393

394

When more than one staff is being used these signs are not always practical. There is, therefore, another set used when the staff cannot be interrupted.

In **395** "B" has a sequence of different movements while "A" repeats one.

396 shows a typical use of this repeat sign when only one part of the body is repeating an action while the rest is moving with different kinds of actions. In this example, action strokes have been used simply to represent action in the rest of the body, while the hand, which is holding a conductor's baton, is repeating a small up/down movement.

397–400 show four adaptations of the basic repeat sign used in **395** and **396** to give a wide range of possibilities.

> **397** shows the sign meaning "repeat on the other side" (*i.e.* do with the left side of the body what you have just done with the right, and vice versa).
> **398** means repeat what "A" is doing now.
> **399** means repeat what you did in bar 27.
> **400** means repeat what "A" did in bar 27, but on the other side.

If a section of the work is to be repeated later, it is named at beginning and end with a letter or Roman figure when it first appears, as in **401**. When the reprise, as it is called, occurs, the same letter or number is used again as in **402**. If it is to be performed including all the lesser repeats that were in the first performance a double diagonal stroke is put in the staff, as in **402a**, but if it is to be performed without the repeats, as is frequently the case with a reprise, then a single diagonal stroke is used, as in **402b**.

A word of warning about the use of repeat signs. While they are a great help to the writer, they can make reading rather complicated, as the reader has to turn back continually to find out what the motifs to be repeated were. It is worth while writing a little more to ease the reader's task and definitely unwise to pepper a score with repeat signs.

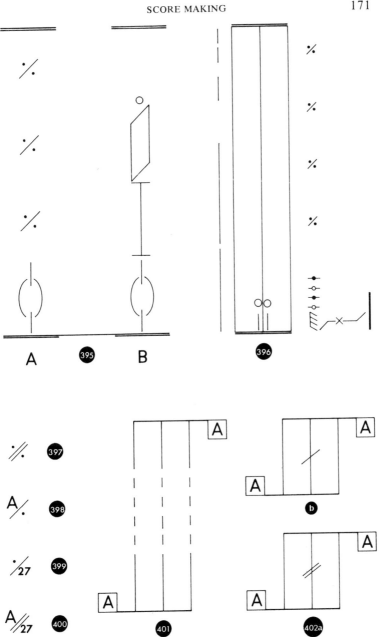

A ⓷⁹⁵ B ⓷⁹⁶

⓷⁹⁷

⓷⁹⁸

⓷⁹⁹

⓸⁰⁰

⓸⁰¹

b

⓸⁰²ᵃ

FLOOR PATTERN GRAPHS AND LAYOUT GRAPHS

In order to make the action as clear as possible to the reader, floor pattern arrangement graphs are drawn for scores of dance. How many there will be is left to the writer's discretion and also where they are put in the score. Colours are used to help differentiate the floor patterns of the various movers, but if this is not possible, which is the case when the score is printed, different kinds of dotted lines can be used instead.

403 shows the standard symbols used to illustrate the beginning front of people or objects and **404** those for their ending front. Any suitable symbols may be used, provided they are clearly identified.

405 shows the floor pattern graph for a couple. The bars to which it refers are written just below the graph.

406 shows a more complicated arrangement graph, where three groups are moving simultaneously. The floor pattern of each group is shown with a different kind of line. Note the opening which represents the proscenium arch.

407 shows a layout graph of a desk.

408 shows a layout graph of a gymnasium.

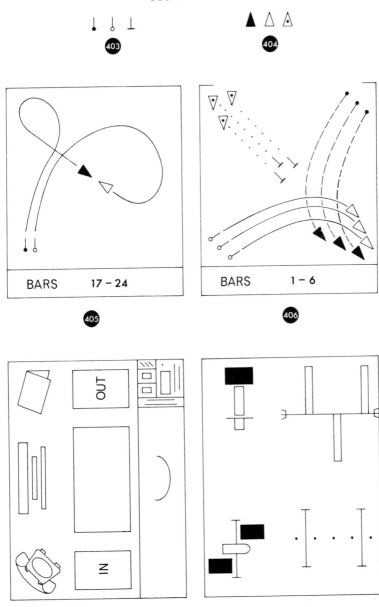

BARS 17 - 24

BARS 1 - 6

TITLES, CREDITS AND COPYRIGHT

It is customary to put various titles on the front page of a score. If it is of a theatre work these are:

(*a*) the name of the work;
(*b*) the name of the creator of the work;
(*c*) the name of the kinetographer and date of writing;
(*d*) the name of the demonstrators;
(*e*) the date and place of the first performance;
(*f*) the title of any music and the name of the composer, and, if possible, the publisher of the musical score.

In fact, credit should be given to anyone responsible for any part of the work, and any information which will be immediately useful to a reader or reconstructor of the work should be included. The dates of the kinetograms are useful historically, as the system will always be developing, and it is helpful, for instance, to know that a work was written before the date of a new form of orthography and can therefore be read with that in mind.

If the kinetograms are medical, industrial or educational the usual titles are:

(*a*) the location (*e.g.* name of hospital or firm or institution and department);
(*b*) the name of the person in charge at location, and of patient, operator, etc.;
(*c*) the name of the kinetographer and date of writing;
(*d*) the purpose of the kinetogram (*e.g.* analysis, records, taxonomy);
(*e*) an identification of any data, collected through any other means, of the movement contained in the kinetogram (*e.g.* film, electro-magneto graphs, force graphs).

Copyright ownership of a kinetogram is a complex question, and will remain so until a court case provides a precedent. Generally speaking, if a kinetographer is paid to write, he should make sure what he is being paid for. He can retain the copyright if he is simply paid by time to record and supply one fair copy. He would then own the pieces of paper and the symbols on them, but not necessarily the right to make copies of the score without permission from his employer. However, the employer might also have to ask the kinetographer's permission to make copies of the score. This is similar to the position of a professional photographer. If the kinetographer is paid to write and hand over the original score (*i.e.* equivalent to the negative of a photograph), then he is also handing over his copyright and should be paid a higher fee. If he writes the score without payment, then he owns all the pieces of paper he has written on. But if he wanted to make copies and sell them, or even give them away, then he would be wise to get some agreement in writing. This is particularly important when the work written is a theatre work or the work of a teacher of, say, folk dance. In these cases the individuals concerned may have put in months or years of creative and research endeavour to produce the work written, and will naturally not be happy to have their work handed round in notation form with no royalty fee.

The known position is that a score of a dance does copyright that dance, so that, say, a dancer in the original choreography cannot produce the same work with other dancers without the permission of the copyright owner. Who this person is is the subject for negotiation, for it may be the impresario, the choreographer or the dance company's director. It is therefore wise always to get some form of agreement in writing before making a score, and clarify what any payment is for.

Chapter Eight

THE PROFESSIONAL KINETOGRAPHER

THE WORK OF KINETOGRAPHERS

A⊤ the time of writing there are only a handful of kinetographers who practise as full-time professionals. These are highly skilled and lengthily trained people who are able to write, read and analyse kinetograms of almost any movement form. But there is a much larger group of fully trained people who choose to use kinetography as an adjunct to some other profession. They may be physiotherapists, psychotherapists, anthropologists, physical education teachers, sports coaches, professional dancers, dance teachers, work study engineers, ergonomists, to name the most popular professions.

Kinetography can therefore be the basic material of a career, or an addition to another career. This situation is a healthy one and likely to continue. It means that there is a two-way process of growth. The system's growth is dependent on information fed to professional kinetographers from people using it practically in specialised circumstances. New demands are made on these people by the impact of technical and artistic developments. The resulting problems can be solved only by enlarging the range of kinetographic descriptions and method. It is dangerous for the system if a specialist creates new rules or signs to suit his own specialism, for, however logical his thoughts may be, they are bound to be coloured by personal preference and pressing circumstances. It is therefore the job of the professional all-round kinetographer to correlate the problems, and solve them in such a way that new orthography is valid for all movement. The new methods are then useful to all writers and the system enriched and made more efficient generally. It is surprising perhaps, but true, that the solution of a problem from work study influences the possible ways of describing a ballet, and vice versa.

Some full-time kinetographers are *freelance*. While this is hazardous from the point of view of a steady income, it enables the kinetographer to work in different fields of movement study. As the furtherance of movement understanding is generally the interest of such a person, the work is satisfying, although economically unstable. Other full-time kinetographers are *employed* by notation centres, by government departments, or by theatre companies and schools. These full-time posts are not common, but work is available in the United Kingdom, some European countries and the U.S.A. At the moment work for a government department is available only in Eastern European countries, where kinetography is used in connection with the recording of folk dance. The work may entail travelling to collect folk dances by watching them being performed in villages, or it may mean working as a link between a collector and a folk-dance company, who perform choreographed ballets based on authentic material. Or it may mean research through the analytical comparison of one dance phrase with another using kinetograms from film.

TRAINING TO BE A KINETOGRAPHER

Full-time training as a kinetographer is available at four centres, to the knowledge of the writer. They are: the Notation Bureau, New York; the Kinetography Department attached to the Folkwang Hochschule in Essen; the Beechmont Movement Study Centre in Kent; and privately under Ann Hutchinson in London. Other Fellows of the International Council of Kinetography Laban may offer full-time training, but there are no other training institutes that are widely used.

Correspondence courses are obtainable up to a fairly high standard of competence, but it is necessary to attend a centre for the advanced-level studies, where individual tuition is given.

The time it takes to become a professional varies with the individual's ability and background. To deal with *ability* first, there is no doubt that a particular kind of mind is required. While many people become competent readers, fewer become fully versatile writers. The ability to observe well and to translate the observed image into symbol speedily requires concentration, an objective outlook, capacity to see detail and to discern the essential from the incidental. Students master the symbols with no difficulty, for these are sensibly thought out and can be assimilated with understanding. The stumbling block for a student is never the symbols but rather his own brain's ability or inability to transmit the image from the retina via the thought processes, to the hand, at speed.

Thoroughness is needed for making fair copies from the scribbles which are taken during observation. Speed and thoroughness do not often go together in one individual, and it is quite common for kinetographers to work as a team, one having the talent to get the movement down quickly on paper and another able to make a master copy with perfect draughtsmanship, having checked and cross-checked for errors and omissions.

With regard to *background*, previous knowledge of some form of movement is a great help to a student. It is not without significance that the majority of kinetographers have some kind of dance training behind them. It would be understandable if older writers were origin-ally dancers because, until after the Second World War, notation was used almost exclusively in and for dance. However, many younger writers have some dance experience. Although dance may well not have been the avenue through which they first heard about notation, there are few better ways of learning about how the body moves than by moving it, and in dance both large and subtle movement changes are experienced and can be observed. Therefore a trainee is likely to be advised to take part in some form of physical activity if he should start to train without having had much practical experience. How-ever, such things as a good knowledge of kinesiology or precise rhythmicality are just as important as motor sensitivity, and it is perfectly possible to become a kinetographer without also being a practical mover.

SPECIALISATION

It has been mentioned that kinetographers sometimes work in teams. This implies specialisms, and there are sufficient practitioners now for specialists to begin to emerge. Kinetographers are on the whole either good writers and passable readers or good readers and passable writers. From the *readers* are developing two types of specialists. The first is the *analyst*. He needs to be a person whose abilities lie in extracting data from kinetograms. This type of work is useful in research where motor skills and disorders are studied. The work is likely to be connected with either medical or industrial research, and, to date, consists in comparative analysis, taxonomy and the preparation of computer-compatible data. The type of kinetogram used in this work is extremely detailed, and not intended for reconstruction into movement, but rather to contain as many facts about the movement as possible.

The second type of specialist reader is the interpreter or *reconstructor*. Such a person has to be able to elicit from the symbols the purpose, function, meaning and expression described by them and to be able to convey this to others either by performing the movement written or by causing others to perform it. These are comparable to musical readers, who convey written notes by playing an instrument or by conducting an orchestra or choir. A reconstructor works almost exclusively in dance and drama. This kind of specialism is developing particularly in the theatre in the U.S.A. and in dance education in the United Kingdom. In the latter the reconstructor is likely to be called upon to produce from a motif writing score. He has to be able to cause other people to choreograph from the freedom of the simple staff score, or be able to choreograph from it himself. Dance experience is very necessary for this sort of work, as is also either a flair for spurring others to creativity or practice as a creative artist. It is likely that when there are more people becoming reconstructors there will be a subdivision into motif writing and full kinetography specialists, for the two require rather different talents.

Specialist *writers* are also emerging. Usually this occurs through knowledge in depth of a limited range of movement. It is likely that this kind of specialist is using kinetography as an addition to another profession. For instance, a kinetographer who is a work study engineer in the electronics industry is likely to be well versed in observing, and describing, minutely detailed finger movements. He is unlikely to be equally good at describing footballers or judo exponents or swimmers in detail. He will know the symbols but not be practised in looking at movements of the whole body, nor familiar with the techniques of sport and the "jargon" used.

Another form of writer who is clearly different from the general practitioner is the writer who uses the simple staff only, *i.e.* the motif writer. To read motif writing is very easy indeed, but to write it well is not. Unfortunately, it is very easy to be a very bad motif writer. This is because the writer's understanding of movement has to be well developed so that he can select the essential features of an action sequence from the incidentals. It is also necessary to be knowledgeable about the kind of movement being written, its purpose, motivation, end product, etc., and to know the purpose of writing it down.

It is obvious that one movement can be described in several ways in motif writing. For instance: a rugger player jumps, stretching up, nearly reaching the ball, with hands leading the way. What should the motif writer select? If he has no knowledge of the game he may write any of the four attributes of the action. If he has no idea of the purpose of the kinetogram he will also be at a loss as to choice of description. The point of the game is to get the ball before anyone else gets it, and therefore a motif writing of the purpose will describe an action towards the ball with a relationship of "near to" the ball as the aim. However, if the purpose of the motif writing is to investigate, say, the nature and number of contractions and extensions in sport, then the very stretched body position will be written and nothing else. The motif writer's observation must therefore be disciplined, through clarity of purpose. When the purpose of the kinetogram is known before observing a movement few difficulties arise.

What is less easy is the description of the essentials of a dance. There are not clear purposes as there are in a sporting event. What have to be found out are the basic themes of the dance, so that their variations, developments, inversions, etc., can be recognised. The ideal is for the choreographer himself to be the writer, for he should know what he is doing. Unfortunately, this does not always function, for two reasons. Firstly, because choreographers are often not trained writers, and secondly, because choreographers do not always know why they have created what they have, or its theme. However, the clarification of an improvisation, or an instinctively created dance, can be greatly helped by writing a motif writing score of it. Passages which are misconstructed or lack meaning or do not fit in with the overall pattern, or whatever, stand out. The choreography can then be gone through, this and that bar or gesture or relationship or direction be altered, until the desired creation is clear both on paper and in the moving bodies. A bad motif writer is one who does not discipline his observation and choice of symbols. He thereby misses the point, and misrepresents the choreography.

STANDARD EQUIPMENT

The following is a list of equipment which every professional needs.

TOOLS FOR GENERAL WRITING

(a) *Pencils*, top grade, HB, B and 2B. Soft pencils are much better than hard, as they are easy to sharpen to a fine point, can be erased without leaving an indentation and blacken well.

(b) *Rubbers*. Rubbers which are transparent help accurate erasing. Those that can be cut to a fine edge with a razor are best.

(c) *Transparent 6-in. and 12-in. rulers*. Rulers with $\frac{1}{16}$-in. divisions are no use on a $\frac{1}{10}$-in. grid paper, although this is the most common division. Transparency is essential. The 12-in. ruler is needed for drawing staffs and the 6-in. more convenient for sign drawing. Centimetre division is needed for European kinetograms.

(*d*) *Pencil sharpener.* Pencil sharpeners which have two holes are best, one for cutting the wood and one for the lead. Some have containers attached, and this is very useful for location writing.

(*e*) *Sandpaper block.* Fine sandpaper is the best stuff for keeping a pencil really sharp. A piece, say 1 in. × 2 in., glued to a piece of wood, is a useful tool.

(*f*) *Draughtsman's pens.* There are various brands of pen on the market. The best type is one which has a detachable holder, each head having an ink container as well as a nib of particular size. Heads of 0·3, 0·4, 0·6 and 0·8 are the most useful sizes. 0·4 makes a good basic size, 0·3 for finer work or small signs, 0·6 and 0·8 for blacking in and motif writing. For every make of pen there is a recommended ink to use, and it is wise to use it. Black is sufficient.

(*g*) *Razor blades.* One-sided razor blades are used for scratching out inked symbols from transparent paper. If an error is made, either make the correction over the error before scratching out or make the correction on the back of the paper. Once scratched, the paper will not take fine ink work. The ink will spread and make a fuzzy effect.

(*h*) *Coloured pencils.* Top-grade coloured pencils are needed for floor pattern drawings and helpful distinguishing marks in scores for several people. Only use the type which can be sharpened to a fine point and do not crumble.

(*i*) *Trace ellipses.* Ellipse curves can be bought for pencil or ink work. The ink ones can be used for both, and are therefore the better buy. They are used for drawing all curves. Two sizes are recommended, 20° and 35°, as between them, these two tracings cover the majority of curve sizes needed.

(*j*) *Compass.* A compass is used in floor-pattern diagrams, and one that will take a pen is recommended.

PAPER

(*a*) *Foolscap blocks of plain bond.* Plain bond paper is needed for location writing. A writer cannot look at the paper while looking at a moving body. It is therefore not possible to write within a staff and watch simultaneously. The jottings on the plain paper are then redrawn on the staff. For motif writing, plain paper is very useful. Pads are better than sheets, because of the hard surface made by the cardboard backing.

(*b*) *Foolscap blocks of graph paper*, with $\frac{1}{10}$-in. grid.

(*c*) *Double foolscap*, with $\frac{1}{10}$-in. grid, in sheets.

(*d*) *Foolscap blocks of plain transparent paper.*

(*e*) *Foolscap blocks of transparent paper*, with $\frac{1}{10}$-in. grid.

$\frac{1}{10}$-in. squared graph paper is the standard paper used for kine-tography. It is not easily obtainable, as most manufacturers add a darker line at the inch and half inch. These rarely coincide with the staff lines. Specially printed paper is available by special order from most good manufacturers, and from all notation centres. Double foolscap size is needed for scores with a large number of movers. The colour of the grid is important. In photographic printing processes blue disappears while black remains, and sepia and red become black. Therefore if the grid is required for the end product black or sepia is the best grid colour. Transparent grids are used for dye-line reproduction, and the same principle applies for colour. Blue-grid transparent paper is not obtainable. The best method to adopt is to use plain transparent paper pinned to a gridded paper so that the staff and symbols can be accurately drawn. The transparent master copy will then reproduce without a grid.

(*f*) *Paper ready printed with staffs.* This type of paper, on a $\frac{1}{10}$-in. grid, is obtainable from notation centres. This is specially ordered and lithographed.

Foolscap size, 13 in. × 8 in., is not an international size of paper. Most European countries use a size between quarto and foolscap.

EQUIPMENT FOR LARGE-SCALE WORK, WALL CHARTS, PRINTING

(*a*) *Letraset, or equivalent, for headings.* Letraset stencils, etc., of letters and numbers are readily available. They are used for headings, bar numbers and any letter or number which appears in a score. There are two types, one for dye-line reproduction and one for general use.

(*b*) *Special Kinetography Letraset.* Beechmont Movement Study Centre have had made, through Letraset, special kinetography tapes with symbols of normal size. These are used for master copies, and are time-saving as well as accurate.

(*c*) *Large sheets of transparent paper.* These are needed for the double-sized publishing kinetograms.

(*d*) *Transparent angle arm.* The V-shaped signs are most easily drawn with an angle arm. This adjusts to whatever angle size is needed, according to the length of the symbol. Transparency is essential.

(*e*) *6-foot rule or equivalent.* Long rules are needed for drawing staffs on wall charts.

(*f*) *T rule.* This is needed for getting the right-angle for bar lines.

(*g*) *Black felt pens or black wax chalks.* Felt pens are used for drawing wall charts. Three sizes are helpful, for fine and medium drawing and for blacking in. There are several kinds of felt pen, some using ink and some "chalk." Some inks tend to spread on the paper, making fuzzy symbols, and some inks are indelible. The non-indelible, non-spreading types are best. These are found by trying out the pen in the shop. The "chalk"-filled pens are not easily available in wide sizes, but are the most reliable for fine work. Wax chalks are good on cheap paper.

(h) *Rolls of paper.* Wallpaper lining is cheap for wall charts, but tends to "spread" the ink. Better paper is recommended for charts intended to last a long time. Wax chalk is good on lining paper, but the chalks are difficult to sharpen to a fine point.

MECHANICAL AIDS

(a) *Oral records.* A portable metronome is used to aid the recording of timing. It is used in conjunction with a tape recorder. The metronome is set, the setting being noted, and runs while the movement is being watched. The tick is recorded on the tape and total time calculated. This is easier to handle than a stop-watch, but less portable. Therefore a stop-watch is more often used on location. On to the tape can also be recorded other sounds which indicate the start or finish of an action. A series of bell-push arrangements which record differently pitched sounds is helpful, but this is a sophisticated arrangement needed only in analytical work. None of these devices is needed for dance with music, as the bar lines, time signatures and beats provide the necessary information.

(b) *Visual records.* 8/16-mm. film cameras, projectors and specto analysers are needed for analytical work. They are expensive, but most professional kinetographers have access to equipment of this type through a firm or university. A film of movement is needed when the movement is to be performed once only, and data is required about it. It is usually needed only in research circumstances.

APPENDIX I

DYNAMICS

N.B. In the last few years the orthography of the dynamic aspect of movement has expanded enormously, and continues, at the time of writing, to expand further. These developments mean that anything written as a comprehensive survey of dynamic descriptions may well be out of date by the time the reader has access to this material. New measuring devices, increased knowledge of body dynamics and kinaesthetic perception, are the factors mainly responsible, and research is currently in progress to further the findings already made. For this reason, dynamics has been put into this Appendix and will be treated very briefly.

TIMING

Kinetography has the vertical dimension of the page for time, and, as a movement notation, is unique in this. *Duration* of change as the basic factor of timing is taken care of by lengthening and shortening symbols. This has been dealt with in Chapter One.

(a) *The time unit.* This is indicated by:
(i) time signature, bar lines, and beat strokes for metric rhythms;
(ii) a time scale on the left of the staff for non-metric rhythms (*see* Appendix V).

(b) *Tempo.* This is shown by a metronome indication, when applicable, and the usual musical tempo indications of *adagio, allegro,* etc., for dance. The time unit is identified in 0·1 second, or larger or smaller units as applicable, for non-metric work, where absolute time is wanted, as well as the relative time taken by each part of the movement.

(c) *Acceleration and deceleration.* These can be shown by the musical method, usually written on the right side of the staff. The rate of acceleration, as calculated by an accelerometer, can be written, if applicable, in numerical form. Other methods are "effort symbols" (*see* this Appendix, **16–22**) or "linear effort graphs" (*see* this Appendix, **23**). Acceleration and deceleration are visible in any kinetogram in a general way, by the increasing or decreasing length of the symbols.

TENSION, FORCE, PRESSURE

The first method used to indicate tension, force or pressure is by *wedge-shaped symbols*. The empty sign (**1**) means "little strength," the blackened symbol (**2**) meaning "more than average strength." These signs are coloquially called *accent signs*, which is inaccurate, but convenient at this stage. Accent signs are written beside movement indications to show the moments when a marked discharge of energy is evident. Their use is as follows:

(*a*) The wedge written vertically means that the part of the body producing the energy is not known, or is irrelevant, or open to choice, or general, according to the context.

(*b*) The wedge tilted to point towards the centre indicates that the part of the body is known. In the full staff the column will show which part, and in the simple staff either a body sign will be written or, if there is no body sign, the accent refers to the right or left side of the body, the part or whole of the side being open to choice.

(*c*) The placing of the wedge has timing significance in relation to the movement sign. The accent can be at the beginning or end or at any point between the two.

(*d*) Increase and decrease of energy are shown by using V and inverted V signs.

(*e*) Maintaining a stated strength is shown by inserting the wedge into a bracket.

Examples of the use of accent signs are shown in **3–6.**

3 shows energy output at the beginning of an action; evident energy but slight in the middle of the action, produced by part or whole of the right body side; marked energy with the left side as the culmination of an action, which is held; marked energy by both body sides.

4 shows a strong clap; the wedges point towards the touch.

5 shows a strong hands touch; the wedges point towards the hands.

6 shows a stamp, a high step with slight tension, three steps and a pause, with increasing strength, diminishing strength on the deepening supporting and slight tension maintained over the high steps, the pause being without particular dynamics.

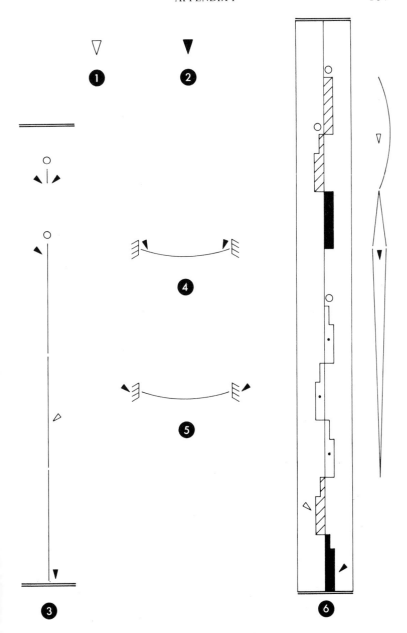

The second method is by using the "*effort*" *symbols*. **7** shows the complete effort notation unit, which consists of lines attached to a diagonal stroke. The line referring to force or energy is shown in **8, 9** meaning "with marked force" and **10** "with lightness" or very slight tension. The exact words to use to describe these states vary according to the type of movement being written, because what is suitable in gymnastics, for example, is unsuitable in dance. A psychologist may regard "force" as a technical term which has quite a different meaning from that given by a biomechanic. What is meant, always, by these symbols is that more or less energy is experienced by the mover. Effort symbols are used:

(*a*) independently of a kinetogram to describe nothing but the dynamics of a movement;
(*b*) beside a kinetogram;
(*c*) in the simple staff to describe when and for how long the dynamics occur, either with or without movement indications.

11 is the method of showing that strength appears and disappears, **12** that strength is included as the main ingredient of the motion experience and **13** that strength must be constantly maintained. **12** and **13** are the most commonly used. **14** shows the effort strength unit in practice.

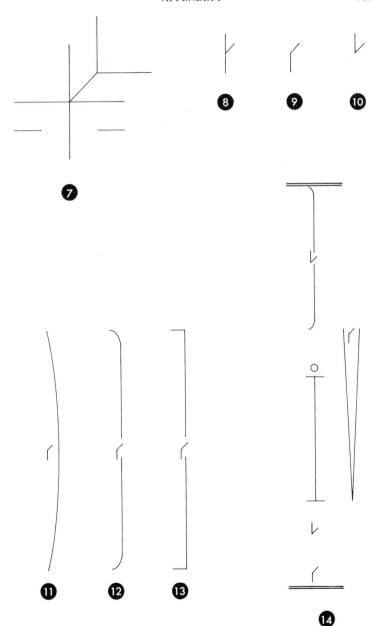

The third method used is called *"linear effort graphs."* There is normally a five-part scale for amount, and the strength changes are plotted on this graph and given time value. (The letters **a–e** are not normally written, but have been put in for explanation purposes only.) In **15**, **c** is the middle state of body tension, average tension, where changes are not perceivable, although known to be taking place; **d** is for evident strength; **e** for marked strength. If the strength line extended beyond **e** it would indicate such a degree of tension that cramped stillness would occur. Scale **b** is for evident light tension, just sufficient to overcome gravity, and **a** for less than adequate tension, relaxed. If the line extended beyond **a** total flop would occur.

15 reads: tension increases from average in two spurts, lessens to be maintained as adequate to overcome gravity, *i.e.* experienced as lightness, increases in strength markedly and, more gradually, increases further until the point of cramp is nearly reached, and is released very quickly to a complete flop. A linear effort graph can stand alone or be written beside a kinetogram describing the actions which accompanied the tension changes.

To return to timing, the effort lines for time are shown in **16, 17** and **18, 17** being slow and **18** quick. These signs describe the moments when slow or quick are experienced, which are likely to be identical with moments of deceleration and acceleration. **19–22** show the combination of tension and timing describable in effort units. **19** is strong and slow, **20** is strong and quick, **21** is light and slow, **22** is light and quick.

The time element can also be written as a linear graph. The grid divisions would mean, **a** very slow, **b** slow, **c** average speed, **d** quick, **e** very quick. Beyond **a** is "stop" and beyond **e** is vibration. Time L.E.G.'s can be very accurate, through measuring instruments, and the subdivisions **a–e** can be clarified to absolute speeds. This is done in laboratory work, but the five-degree scale is usually sufficient if this graph expresses what is experienced only and not what actually occurs in detail. In **23** a dotted line is used for time and has been added to the force line of **15**.

FLOW, CONTINUITY AND CONTROL

A movement flows on when one part of it leads straight into the next with no break. This is seen in kinetograms by the overlap of timing in general, and by the absence of any gaps and retention signs to indicate that movement ceases. However, it is sometimes necessary to say that fluidity of movement is essential, or its opposite, restriction and control. These two poles of flow are very fine shades

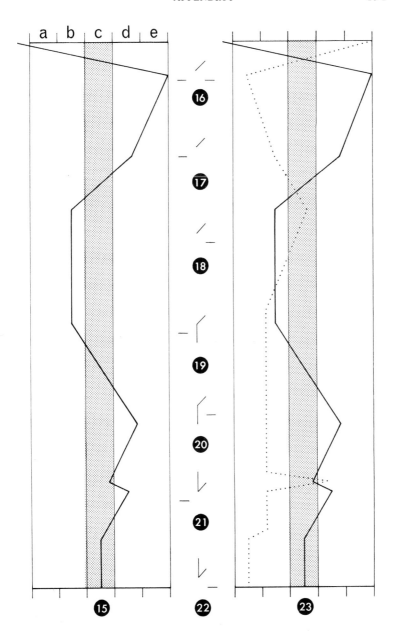

of force/time/body-use rhythms, most easily appreciated by the indication "flow on" or "do not flow on."

Four methods exist:

(a) Words.

(b) Phrasing brackets to link the actions which flow continuously one after the other (**24**).

(c) Effort units (**25–27** and **31**).

(d) Linear effort graphs (**32**).

SPATIAL CONTROL

Spatial pattern is completely clear in a full kinetogram. However, the need to express how a movement is aimed and controlled in space does arise. The means are as follows:

(a) Words.

(b) Effort units (**28–30**).

(c) Linear effort graphs (**32**).

24 shows a simple phrase in which a triangular shape is performed twice. Because the angles between the three movements are acute, there is likely to be a slight break in the flow of the movement. In order to show that the second time the shape is made the three parts must flow on, a phrasing bow is used.

25–30 show the effort units for flow and space.

25 is the flow line.

26 is restricted in flow.

27 is freely flowing.

28 is the space line.

29 is linear spatial use.

30 is plastic spatial use.

Varying words are used to describe these effort units according to their context.

31 shows two people about to shake hands. Beside are written two possible flow indications. The restricted movement is typical of people who do not want to shake hands. Tiny movements of withdrawal hardly describable, yet discernible, will be present. Free flow is typical of friends meeting; their tiny movement differences are described by an effort unit.

32 shows the linear effort graphs of the hands of two workers using scissors to cut a circular piece of paper. Worker A uses one motion, worker B several smaller ones. Note the simplified layout of the L.E.G.'s, which is customarily used when they are drawn on graph paper. (*See* Appendix V, **49**, for further illustrations of dynamics.)

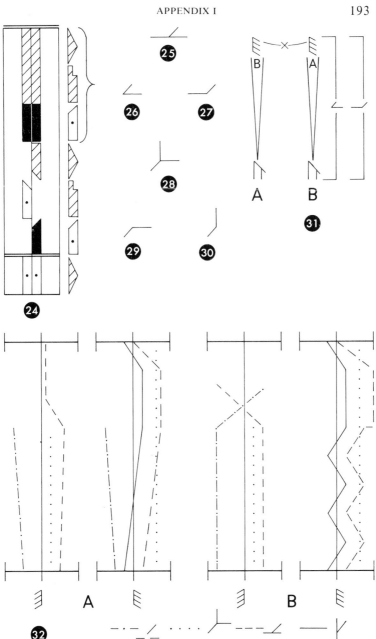

24 25 26 27 28 29 30 31
A B
32 A B

APPENDIX II

SPECIAL NEEDS FOR WRITING SWIMMING

N.B. The standard sign for water in internationally used kinetograms is A in a square (*see* **334**) but in those written for English-speaking readers the more easily understood W in a square is customary.

In **33** the carrying sign is written completely across the staff and attached to the symbol for water. This device is used to show that the whole body is supported by the water.

34. This means floating on the stomach.

35. This means floating on the back.

36. This means floating on the side.

37. This is a general indication for **34–36** respectively.

38. Here progression in the water is shown by a path sign.

39. Here the head is lifted out of the water. It is shown by a touch sign, from above, attached to the sign for water surface.

40. This shows standing on the bottom of the bath or sea with the water surface at waist level.

41. This shows walking on the bottom with the water up to shoulder level, then floating on the stomach.

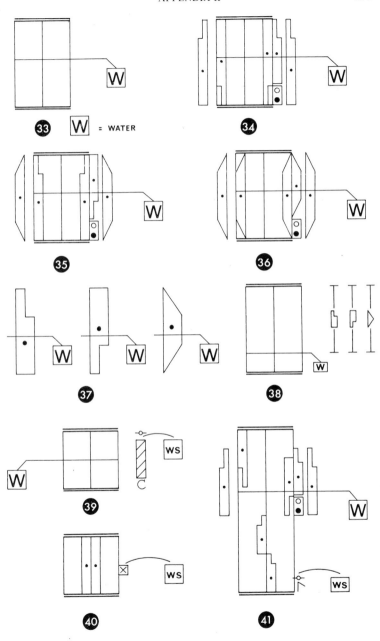

33   W = WATER

34

35

36

37

38

39

40

41

APPENDIX III

NOTES ON WRITING GYMNASTICS

THE gymnast must first decide on drawings which will represent the various pieces of apparatus to be used. The drawings on the opposite page (**42**) are examples, but others may be chosen, probably in connection with a particular textbook. The "pictures" are written beside the kinetograms. If one at a time is used they are usually drawn on the right side (**43**). In a sequence using more than one piece each piece has a column of its own (**44**).

The order in which kinetography is given to students of gymnastics may be different from that given in this book. The body signs, supports, methods of progression, rotations, partner relationships and apparatus signs will be paramount, while direction, metre, area signs, etc., will be of secondary importance.

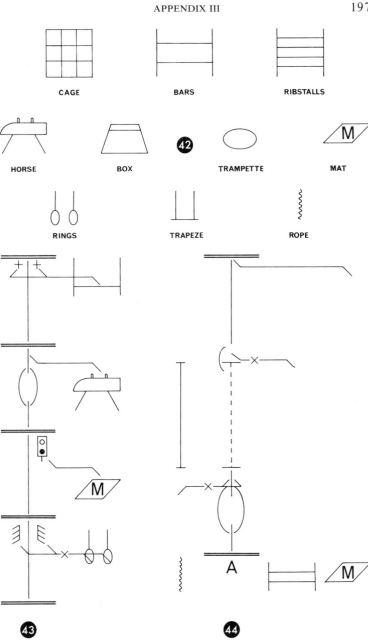

CAGE   BARS   RIBSTALLS

HORSE   BOX   42   TRAMPETTE   MAT

RINGS   TRAPEZE   ROPE

M

M

A   M

43   44

APPENDIX IV

SPECIAL NEEDS FOR GAMES PLAYED ON
A COURT

N.B. The word "court" will be used to represent any marked games area, such as a pitch.

THE recording of skilled actions on a court is usually aided if the directions are related to the axes of the court. This is because the mover is likely to be very aware of these axes and to line up his movements in relation to them. The tennis stroke illustrated in **45** has the steps, turn and racket positions in relation to the court, while the body's movements are written in relation to the trunk. Forwards for the racket and the steps means netwards, sideways means parallel to the net and base line. This is how the movement is most likely to be perceived by the player, as he must be acutely aware of the court layout. This is particularly necessary in squash.

In sports, on a large pitch, the path of the ball is written according to the pitch while the player's movements are written normally. Detailed area signs are essential as the exact positions on the field of the players are vital to the recording.

45 is a kinetogram of maximum detail taken from a film. The amount of detail means that the kinetogram is primarily for comparison purposes and not to be reconstructed, as it contains far more information than can be transmitted to the body.

[Note the small diamond. It occurs in the right leg column, twice, in the left body column and in the left arm column. It is the space retention sign. In each case it modifies a turn or a twist, in that a part of the body is directed, by the sign, not to be carried round by the turn, but to retain the spatial direction in which it is at the beginning of the turn.]

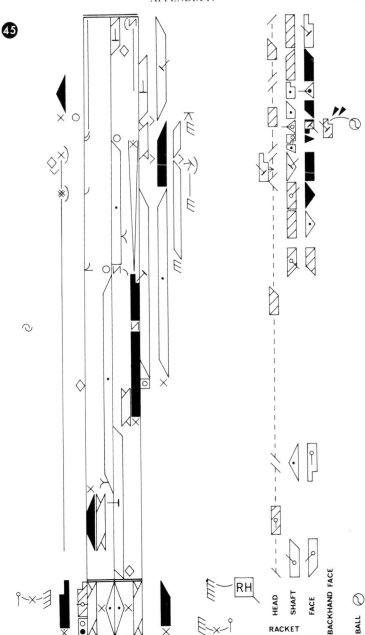

APPENDIX V

NOTES ON INDUSTRIAL WRITING

INDUSTRIAL movement is a wide term embracing movement done for a purpose with objects. It ranges from dealing a pack of cards to working at a complicated factory bench or cleaning a bus. While movements such as shovelling coal or lifting a heavy object involve the whole body, many industrial movements are centred round the hands and lower arms. Especial attention has to be given to these parts, and sometimes extra columns are needed for individual fingers and for the movement of the objects used.

In **46** a rake is gripped by both hands; the right hand is higher up the rake than the left. The rake's direction is shown by two direction signs. It is touching the floor.

The movements are written at first with little or no attention paid to their timing. The notator then decides on a time scale; this may be taken from a stop-watch, a metronome or a number of film frames. It is sometimes sufficient to count by beating a finger in strict metre, fairly quickly. He decides how many units of time are taken by the whole action. Let us say he decides 27. He then notes at the side of the staff the exact moment when each action begins, and how many units each takes. In **47** he has noted that there are recognisable changes in the movement on counts 3, 4, 8, 15, 16 and 21. He draws lines from the count staff to the relevant columns. In the final draft he draws his staff in 27 equal units and then places his symbols correctly, taking into account the moment of start, the duration of the change, the duration of the pause, etc.

In this way the rhythm of two workers doing the same task can be compared, which is often the purpose of industrial writing. It may be necessary, also, to denote the time taken in seconds or minutes. In this case the notator must relate his time units to actual time. In **48** worker B takes 3·0 seconds, worker A takes 2·7 seconds.

If necessary the staff can be abandoned altogether and columns made for any particular parts of the body or objects which have movement. **49** is an excerpt from the action of threading a needle. From left to right the staffs are: Motif Writing; Kinetography; Effort Symbols; and, last, Linear Effort Graph.

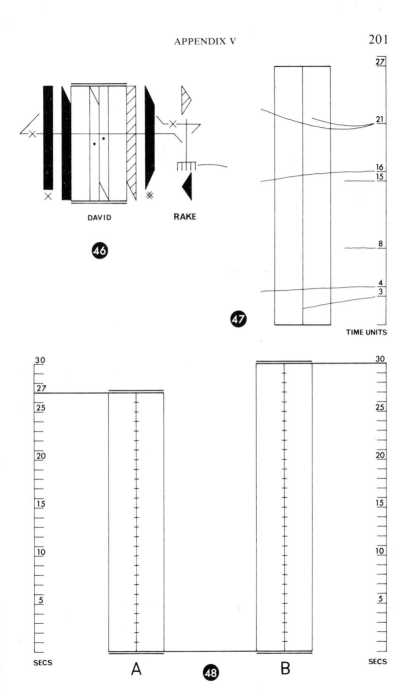

DAVID   RAKE

46

47

TIME UNITS

SECS   A   **48**   B   SECS

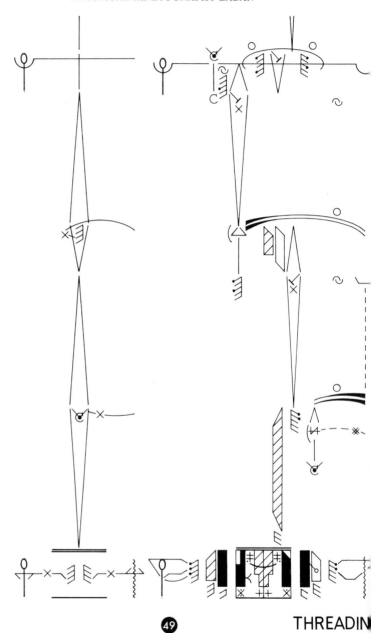

49

THREADIN

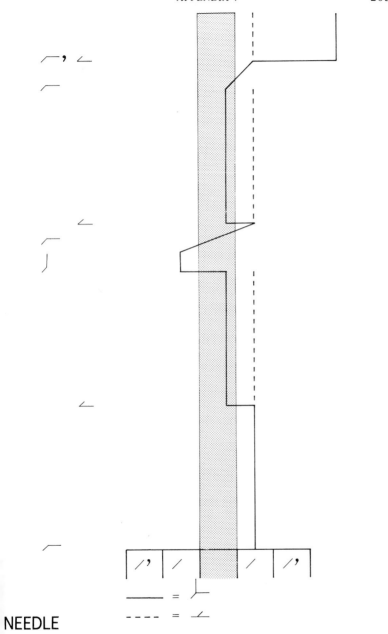

NEEDLE

APPENDIX VI

NOTES ON COMBINING KINETOGRAMS
WITH OTHER GRAPHS

ANY graph with a time scale can be written beside a kinetogram. To correlate, it is necessary to use the same time scale in each. This may mean transposing one or the other, which is a very simple process, causing no problems.

This is likely to be done in research work where information of different kinds about an action is compared or correlated.

The most likely types of graph are:

(a) those recording the aspects of the mechanics of the motion;
(b) those recording the types of perception of the mover;
(c) those assessing the dynamics experienced by the mover;
(d) those recording changes in the function of parts of the body's mechanism during movement.

50 is an example of a jump with a recording of the vertical force of the mover exerted on a force platform.

[Note the sign in the left body column of the starting position. When this sign is written outside the staff, or attached to a turn, it means focal point, as has been explained. However, when in the gesture column of the staff, it means the centre of gravity or centre of weight. In this starting position the weight is directed by the pin sign to be slightly forwards. This is released immediately movement begins.]

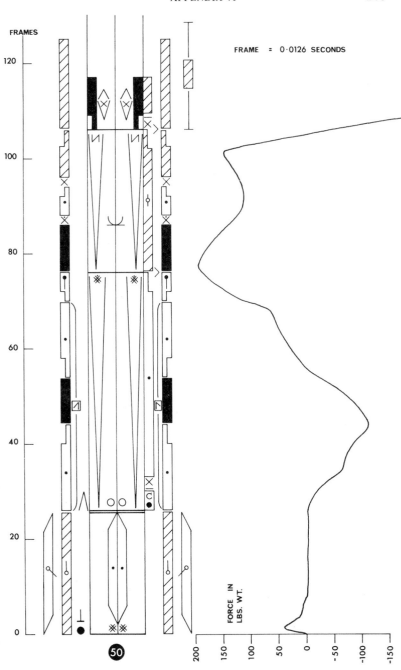

FRAMES

FRAME = 0·0126 SECONDS

FORCE IN LBS. WT.

50

APPENDIX VII

THE USE OF NOTATION IN THE TRAINING OF PHYSICAL EDUCATION AND DANCE TEACHERS

WHERE notation is to be included in a course of training it has been found that the most helpful way of treating the subject is to regard it as a visual aid to the appreciation of the practical movement. On no account should separate notation sessions be given unrelated to practical movement.

Learning the symbols presents no difficulty when the movement task and the relevant symbols age given simultaneously. A student understands both at once as one experience. It is suggested that notation is presented first as symbols, not in a staff at all, very much as reading is presented first as words and later as sentences. The first symbols may well be those for parts of the body. Charts, or diagrams, or handout sheets can be used, and, as the students are made aware of the moving parts of the body, the symbols are pointed out and assimilated. It may be thought that a person of student age would know how the body is put together and that symbols would be superfluous. However, people who have been teaching movement for many years have been amazed to find that the symbols brought to their notice an organisation of the body which is most helpful to progressive bodily articulation.

When movement with a body stress is begun the first "verb" of movement to be written should be simply the action stroke, as in Chapter One of this book. The fact that the body can move as a whole, or parts in isolation, or parts in unison, with parts leading, with parts supporting or with parts related, can easily be shown and brought home to students by introducing the sign for "leading with," and the whole group of signs for relationships. A wealth of vocabulary can then be explored by the student by playing with symbol combination. This can be done with little supervision and enables a student to work on movement tasks by himself or herself in a framework which aids purposeful study. That this approach functions can be accepted only by experience. Again and again, it has been found that ten minutes' introductory class work can be followed by at least two hours' individual work with students working at their own pace.

This enables the staff member to give personal tuition and help. Without the symbols, the time a student can work alone is remarkably diminished, to as little as a quarter of an hour. Without a visual aid the student loses sight of what he has done and loses sense of direction and systematic trial and error, which results in apathetic effort and dissatisfaction. The symbols also aid memory when the work, months later, is to be presented to children. Without symbols a combination of kinaesthetic memory, longhand notes and intellectual memory is all that he can rely on. The symbols provide spurs to memory aid, and the work done is far more easily recalled.

When the practical work is composing with the body as the main theme notation can again aid. Examples of very simply written dances can be read. They need not be reconstructed, but can be read for the purpose of understanding and of seeing examples of ways in which movements can be constructed together. To read and understand the "story" or sequence of events is far easier than reconstructing, as this entails memorising the themes. It has been experienced that using simply notated dance in this way gives a framework for purposeful action. Many students who are afraid to compose by themselves, or positively dislike improvising, find that this introduction gives them confidence to start and a purpose to their trials and errors.

When a composition has been completed the simple staff and very limited groups of symbols can be used to write the theme of what has been made. One should not carry out this exercise merely to get the theme written down, but rather to have a way of assessing the standard of the composition. As dance is ephemeral, criticising it usually entails watching it being performed several times. This takes time, and many points are missed. To have a simple script to study means that purposeless, illogical, themeless moments in the dance are seen as empty spaces in the script, or as the appearance of quite different groups of symbols. It is possible to look critically at one's own dance in this way, a thing which is quite impossible without a script. It has been found that this method enables a student to assess his own work, improve it and feel immense confidence at being able to progress by the aid of his own critical faculties. He is able to assist his colleagues, and there is much less dependence on the staff member. It means also that each person is able to improve his work simultaneously, a thing which is not possible when the staff member is the only one able to give critical assessment.

Whether the work is gymnastics or dance, about action, body management, direction or dramatic interplay, the same methods apply, namely the use of notation as a visual aid to initial learning and critical evaluation. The amount of work done in the same time is enormously increased, as is the workmanlike approach to the subject of movement education.

Should there be concern that notation detracts from the creative or inventive nature of dance and physical education, one can only assure that it does not when handled in this way. The detailed writing in full kinetography of movements created and the reconstruction of full scores certainly does detract. Whether this occurs or not depends on the lecturer's imaginative use of notation as a subject.

How often notation should be part of a movement session depends on the nature of the session. There are obviously times when kinaesthetic appreciation of movement is the main aim of the work, in which case notation would be irrelevant and a distraction. But in any situation where a grasp of material is what is wanted, or assessment of the content of practical work done, notation is relevant and increases student comprehension.

INDEX

References to the diagrams are in bold type; other references are to pages of the text.

25p 23/12/77 (sale price)